MW01121737

Boarding the Baby Boat

A Guide to the Baby Decision

Imogen Barnacle

Barnacle, Imogen

Boarding the baby boat - A guide to the baby decision.

© Copyright 2015. All rights reserved. No part of this publication may be reproduced, transmitted or distributed in any form or by any means, or held in any information storage and retrieval system without the author's prior written permission.

First edition published by Baby Boat Press - 2015

Baby Boat is a registered trademark.

National Library of Australia Cataloguing-in-Publication entry:

Barnacle, Imogen, author.
Boarding the baby boat : a guide to the baby decision /
Imogen Barnacle.

ISBN: 9780994257307 (paperback)

Pregnancy--Decision making.
Pregnancy--Psychological aspect
Parenthood--Psychological aspects.
Family size--Decision making.

612.63

Disclaimer:

This book is intended as an information source only. You use any information provided solely at your own risk. The author assumes no responsibility, whether implied by law or otherwise, for the information provided and disclaims all liability with respect to such information and its usage.

The health advice and opinions in this book are not intended to be nor are they to be treated as a substitute for, or in replace of professional medical help and assistance. If you have any specific medical condition, question or concern always consult your doctor or a medical professional.

For further information relating to motherhood and the baby decision visit:

http://www.babyboat.com.au

http://babyboat.com.au/blog

Dedicated to:

John Richard Bertram

A person who taught me that every single life

can impact upon the happiness of others…

May he rock the heavens!

My family, my daughters and the ones I love

Contents

PART ONE

AN UNEXPECTED JOURNEY BEGINS

Chapter 1

An Unexpected Journey Begins

The big question

Do you remember bubble gum jeans and WHAM T-shirts, but have no idea who on earth Dora is, let alone recognise words to a Wiggles song?

If you overheard someone talking about size zero, would you imagine the conversation to be about some footballer's wife? If so, you are amongst the growing number of women who have cruised through the nineties and naughties on full throttle, totally missing the baby boat. Since you are reading my book today, I can assume you're here because you reached either that all-powerful milestone of thirty-five years of age or a point where the question, *do I want children?* demands a real answer and can no longer be shrugged off with, *maybe one day. I think I need another drink.*

In our twenties, we are just starting out in life—getting our first home, building our careers, and enjoying ourselves every chance we get. Having children is often part of a far-distant view of what our futures may hold. We know without a doubt that having a baby is a massive commitment. And before we even think about starting a family we want to experience life on our own—do some travelling, achieve some of our life goals, and indulge ourselves a little before getting tied down.

For most of us, this approach to life works just fine, and we are able to cruise along. But just when we begin to feel comfortable, our thirties run up and hit us in the back of the head! Suddenly, our ambivalent little lives are disrupted as we realise we aren't getting any younger and we haven't thought about children for quite some time. So what happened? Well, somewhere between our weekend escapes, overseas holidays, and outdoor music festivals, we lost track of time. We became victims of a pesky little guy known as ... the time bandit!

Of course, the last decade or so hasn't been a total waste. If all has gone according to plan, your career is now on a roll, you have started renovating your dream home, managed to meet your other (though not necessarily better) half, and even decided to get married. Like me, you have been having a fabulous time and keeping yourself busy. But no matter how busy you are or how often you avoid the issue, the time will come when you start thinking that something might be missing from your life. You may begin to wonder, *how much longer can it be just the two of us?*

The idea of starting a family may not always be at the forefront of our thoughts, but I'm willing to bet that we can all admit to times when we have thought about children's names, smiled at their cute little outfits, or pictured ourselves rocking a baby to sleep. But in most cases, these daydreams are followed by a thousand questions: *Can we afford it? Would we make good parents? Am I too selfish and set in my ways?* Thinking about parenthood can seem too hard so, instead of dealing with the issue, we push it to the back of our minds and open the paper to the movie guide, thus allowing the tug-of-war to continue.

Whether you have been trying to avoid the subject or not, you must admit that babies are a hot topic. Everywhere you look people are either having babies or talking about kids. And in recent times, we have experienced the biggest baby boom since, well, since the era of the baby boomers. But unlike previous generations for whom having children was as natural as a sunrise, today's potential parents are a little more hesitant and question whether a family is right for them. Up until 'the night that changed my life' (more about that later), my partner Brad and I fell neatly into the latter category. Until 'that evening', we were like most people our age, we were stuck on the proverbial fence and not taking seriously the idea of having a baby.

For me, deciding whether to 'board the baby boat' and have a child of my own was extremely difficult. Actually, it was extremely difficult for us both. Just a few short months before Brad put 'that' question out there, we were both 99.9% sure that we didn't want a family. Now don't get me wrong, we both loved kids. You could take me along to a barbeque with little ones in attendance and I would be off playing with them before you knew it … Okay, as long as I had a cold beer in my hand. But as the day came to a close, I would be happy for all those kids to go home with their parents whilst I stayed and partied, safe in the knowledge that I could sleep until ten the next day if I wanted to.

After eight years together doing our own thing, Brad and I had become like many child-free couples: selfish with our time. We had a way of life and a routine in place that we knew would certainly be interrupted by pregnancy and the addition of small children. At that time, I could have easily written a long list of 'reasons not to' have a baby, and only ever had one item on my 'reasons to' list. Of course it was a momentous one, the doozy of all arguments! You probably have already thought about it a hundred times yourself.

Do you know what that one reason is? Okay, then, here we go. Drum roll, please! The all-powerful and *only* reason I ever had on my list in favour of having a baby was … yes … that's right … here it comes …

If I don't have a baby, will I regret it when I am older?

There, I've said it! It's out in the open. Phew!

Now, let me ask how many of you are looking down at your own list and saying, "This girl is psychic! That is amazing!" Quite a few I imagine.

So, how did all this get started for me? Why did *I* of all people now have to answer this big question?

It all began one warm mid-October night. Brad, my beloved other half and I were sitting in our dining room eating dinner. We were relaxing and catching up on our day whilst the television ran in the background. I was enjoying our mandatory after-work glass of wine when *those words* popped out of Brad's mouth.

'Hey babe, we really should start thinking about whether we want to have kids. We're not getting any younger, you know!'

I almost choked on the spot! (But seriously, do you think I'd waste a drop of good wine by letting it fly out of my nose?)

There it was! Out there! In the atmosphere! Hanging in the air, waiting patiently for a reply! My poor brain, which until then had been happily focusing on its next morsel of food, was all of a sudden forced into a flat spin. Sure, we may have said those words to each other half-heartedly once in a while, but this time something was different. This time those words had a serious edge to them.

I immediately thought, am I supposed to answer that? It sounded a lot like a question, so I guess I am required to say something now!

To break the silence, I used a response that all self-respecting women know—the one best suited to these kinds of situations.

"Hm!" I said.

Question answered. Saved! Back to the wine. Oh, and what's that on the telly?

I let out a giant sigh of relief. The danger had passed and everything was back to normal. Phew!

What? Hang on a minute ... more words were coming. Ahhh! What was happening?

Brad pulled me back into the conversation and, although both of us are procrastinators, I had to admit that the time had come to take the matter seriously. And since I was the one who had to be pregnant and give birth, it seemed that, by default, the choice had to be mine.

In the days that followed *that night*, I faced the hardest and most frustrating decision I have ever had to make. I changed my mind every two hours.

During this time, I watched movies that tugged at the maternal heartstrings, and I would think, *yes, definitely. Let's do it*. But then a few hours later, I'd think about having to give up our Sunday counter lunches or my weekend nanna naps, and I would decide, *no way am I doing that! Absolutely NOT!* It went on like that for weeks.

As the days passed, poor Brad kept asking, 'So what do you think?' I honestly wanted to give him an answer, but I couldn't. I desperately wanted to be twenty-seven again, with a few more years to think about it, but I was fast approaching thirty-six and knew that meant no more pussyfooting around. It was time to make a decision.

Some people may think that if you don't know the answer to the baby question, then either you're not ready or you're not cut out for parenthood. But I am here to tell you from personal experience that this isn't always the case. When I set out on this journey, I was in such turmoil that I openly discussed my dilemma with anyone who would listen—and quickly found that my feelings were not uncommon. They were, in fact, extremely widespread among people my age. It seemed that when it came to having babies, my feelings of doubt, apprehension, and indecisiveness were not exclusively mine.

Whilst it was comforting to know I was not alone in my thoughts, it didn't make my decision any easier. I knew it was a decision that would totally change my life—but for the better or, the worse? There was no way to tell. I only knew that this decision would transform the fundamental way in which I lived and that everything I did and everything I had planned for the future would change.

And not being a big fan of surprises, I was stuck!

Research and the swinging pendulum

Once I came to the realisation that chats with friends were futile and I was never going to make a firm decision on my own, I knew it was time to start my research. And I am famous for doing research. I research *everything* and was sure this hobby of mine would yield great results.

I worked hard and looked everywhere for answers, but it seemed that this time around, effort wasn't going to equal a positive outcome. No matter how much I read or studied, the answer just wasn't out there. As I continued weighing the pros and cons, I would come to a decision I felt confident with ... but then a day, a week, or even five minutes would pass, and I would find myself backtracking.

Deep down, I knew that I didn't need to keep researching. I already knew all the pros and cons. But now that I had to make the right decision, what I needed was some real help, some real information, a real point of view.

What I needed was a book or even an article or two, from the perspective of a person who was just like me, with the same feelings, the same doubts, and the same fears. I desperately needed honest insight into the biggest question I had ever faced in my life. Like most women of my generation, I rarely make life-changing decisions lightly. So, as the pendulum swung back and forth, my search continued.

I googled. I blogged. I pounded the library aisles. Alas, my literary search went unrewarded. I couldn't find a single piece of information to help me.

Most 'born mummies' are under the impression that when the time comes, you 'just know'. For them, entering into motherhood is a perfectly natural progression, so they often don't understand why other women need guidance.

But for me, and other women who don't have those maternal clocks that just switch on, motherhood is a decision that has to be made.

The pros and cons

To help me on my journey from hard-partying rock princess to mummy and child advocate, I created a now-notorious and exhaustive list of pros and cons. Do any of these items sound familiar?

Cons:

Pregnancy: the sickness, the rules, the weight gain, and the constant tests;

Labour: pain, pain, and more pain;

Giving up drinking and socialising;

Finances: cost to be pregnant, raising the child, time off work and over the long term;

Schools: child care, high school, university;

Spending Saturdays driving to sport and dance classes;

Making Easter hats at 11 pm when someone forgets to tell you she needed it for the parade the next day;

No more freedom to do things when we want;

No more sleep, sleep-ins, or hangovers;

Spending the weekend at parks and parties at McDonald's;

No overseas travel, no backpacking, no weekends away;

No concerts or sitting in the pub watching a band;

Babysitter required in order to do anything;

Having to pack a million bags to do anything;

Worrying about someone all the time;

Living in mess and chaos;

Having someone reliant on you 24/7;

Dealing with a baby, a toddler, a teenager, and all the relative behaviours and problems;

Doubting if we are emotionally or physically ready; and

A thousand other reasons.

Pros

If we don't have children, will we regret it?

With a list like this, you may be wondering why soul searching was ever necessary; it seems quite clear that my mind had already been made up. And before that balmy October night, I genuinely thought it was. But what I discovered on this journey is that I am, after all, a mere human and a female one at that. Like it or not, my thoughts and feelings are still strongly governed by some basic human instincts, particularly the maternal instinct itself. When I look back, I think, *honestly, did I really stand a chance?*

Feeling maternal and the contemplation of motherhood

There seems to be a social expectation that women should naturally feel maternal, that having a child is perfectly normal and we all cannot wait to jump into motherhood. Thanks to these social beliefs and expectations, it can be hard enough for women to publicly discuss their doubts about entering into parenthood, let alone suggest they don't want children at all.

People usually have strong views about family, which can sometimes make women feel as if they are betraying the 'Institute of Motherhood' by voicing doubts on the subject. Women who are unsure about having children often feel judged as weird or freaks of nature. Consequently, they either secretly wonder if they are entitled to their own opinions and feelings or decide it's safer to keep quiet on the subject. This attitude creates an enormous problem for women, who may feel they have no opportunity to discuss their feelings openly and honestly without fear of backlash and criticism. These women are likely to be left confused and with many questions unanswered.

Historically, societies often based a woman's worth on her ability and desire to reproduce. Over the past decade or so, there has been a drastic change in women's focus and attitude, particularly women from Generation X, the offspring of the baby boomers. These women are the daughters of the first real 'Women's Libbers' and, thanks to their mothers, see the world through remarkably different eyes to those of previous generations. The influence of our mothers has ensured that we have grown up to believe that when it comes to life, we have choices. And it's thanks to these brave parents and the wider acceptance and availability of contraception that we have become the first generation of women who have contemplated 'not' having children. We are the first ones to be brought up to believe that children, marriage, and motherhood are actually options and not givens. We have been raised to believe that when it comes to childbearing, 'just because you can, doesn't necessarily mean that you should'.

This attitude has allowed many of us to cruise through our lives confident in our ability to make decisions and never doubting ourselves because we usually know exactly what we want and how to get it. But when that all-powerful, life-changing number 'thirty-five' starts to move closer or even passes us by, often things can change. Many of us begin to second-guess ourselves, our decisions, and our life goals. For strong confident women, this sudden imbalance can make many of us feel vulnerable and uncertain.

As women, we know that we have an internal biological clock that ticks, and we know what that ticking clock means, but that doesn't mean this information isn't frustrating. We may even feel angry that the biggest decision we will ever have to make has been largely taken out of our hands by the big guns themselves: Time and Mother Nature. And the realisation that the clock will not tick forever can bring us to a place of doubt and, worse, fear that we might miss the baby boat and our chance at motherhood. We begin to wonder if we will be left to suffer the inexplicable loss of what could have been.

Have reached the point where you finally think it's time to answer the questions: *Do I feel maternal?* and *Do I really want children?* If so, then you should address the issue the same way in which you have approached every other significant decision in your life: sensibly, and with a wealth of knowledge and facts to support you.

When I commenced this journey, what I really needed was to understand the motivation for having children. The women I pestered with questions told me that yes, motherhood was hard but no, they wouldn't change things for the world, but I needed something more. As time passed I began to wonder if these mothers were even capable of giving me the information and insight I craved. Would I ever get any helpful answers beyond the usual 'It's good, just different'. They were parents, after all, and I didn't think my questions were that difficult:

What is pregnancy really like?

If you knew then what you know now, would you still have gone through with it?

Is motherhood really all it's cracked up to be?

Do you regret your decision to have children?

Surely, I thought, these women could remember life before children and tell me the truth. I kept wondering if they were afraid of being honest with me for fear that their frankness would make it look like they didn't love their children. I just didn't know.

And just to make matters worse, I always think long term. Sure, I knew there would be morning sickness and toddler tantrums in the beginning, but what kept me up at night was worrying about how I would deal with life later on. How would *I* deal with a teenage pregnancy or a 3:00 am phone call telling me my son had been arrested for drink driving in his mate's car? I knew I was over-thinking things, but I couldn't help it. To become a mum myself, I needed to have my fears taken away. I needed my friends to tell me that I had nothing to worry about and that it all works out in the end! I needed reassurance.

When I looked at my friends and their lives, I just couldn't work out if I was like them, or if I could become like them. I loved kids, but I didn't have that natural 'mothering instinct' some women are born with. The idea of being pregnant and giving birth had never appealed to me. I had never dreamt of holding a baby in my arms or fantasised about watching one grow. Even at school, I didn't share my classmates' dreams of getting married and having children. Like all kids, I had plans for my future; they just didn't involve a family.

Getting started

Whether you feel a maternal instinct or not, the first thing you need to do when making a decision of this magnitude is to sit down and honestly assess what you want out of life. Not only what you want now but, since it takes at least eighteen years to raise a child, what you may want to achieve over the next twenty years. Some of the fundamental questions you should start exploring include:

> How do I see my future?
>
> What are my specific goals or plans?
>
> How important are these goals?
>
> Can they be put on hold?
>
> Can or will these plans include a family?

In this book, I present questions for you and your partner to explore together. I also provide you with opinions, advice, and insight into how things are, and were, for me during the process and beyond.

I understand that this decision is not easy and that there are many questions you and your partner need to ask yourselves; however, I do think there is no better place to start this journey than right at the beginning. So, understanding what you want out of life is an essential first step.

Of course, most of us would probably agree that we want to be happy, healthy, and successful in life. We want to have the freedom to pursue the things we love, and the time we need to enjoy them. Maybe we would like to travel the world, afford the latest fashion, and enjoy nice dinners out.

But when posing this question to yourself, you actually need to think about the core, or fundamental, parts of your life: the simple, vital parts that are important to you. These include:

Having enough time to spend with the people you love;

Which parts of your current life are non-negotiable that you want to keep;

What compromises you are willing to make.

The next step is to think about your future. You will need to use your imagination to think about how your life would be both with children and without. Close your eyes and visualise both scenarios, and then use these scenarios to review the different kind of future each alternative holds. Are there elements of both lifestyles that you would enjoy or look forward to? Or does one lifestyle look better or worse than the other?

Also ask yourself lifestyle questions, such as:

Have I partied enough?

Do I enjoy nights at home with a good bottle of wine and a DVD?

Do I enjoy having a few friends over for dinner or an afternoon barbeque instead of hitting the clubs and the Sunday sessions?

If you are down to a few big nights out a year, and Saturday evenings at home no longer seem so bad, then you may have discovered one of the first compromises you are prepared to make in order to become a parent.

What I have found since having a family is that whilst my life certainly has changed, it isn't necessarily better or worse. It is more about how I live and experience it that has changed. So when thinking about how you will be spending *your* future leisure time, imagine what it would be like to spend Saturday mornings at cricket matches and ballet lessons, rather than catching an early wave with your mates. Right now this might seem like a no-brainer to you, after all how could spending time with a child be as enjoyable as your current recreational activities? I thought the same thing, but then discovered that it actually *is* just as enjoyable. And I've discovered that the compromises and lifestyle changes I have undergone are not the sacrifices I believed they would be.

Whilst I do sometimes miss my old life and the freedom and choices it offered, I don't miss it nearly as much as I expected. And yes, there are times when I feel a pang of jealousy when I see a group of carefree twenty-somethings laughing as they walk into their local bar or café. But as a mother, I now feel a real purpose in my life and a renewed sense of energy and excitement about my future. If I walked into that bar with those twenty-somethings, I'd feel like I was missing out on spending that time with my daughter. And even though motherhood means I am not doing *all* the things I used to enjoy, once my daughter was out of the infancy stage, I began doing many of the things I used to—it's just the *how* and *when* that is different.

For example, I still go to the beach for a holiday every year. But instead of baking on the sand and hiking through rainforests, I now enjoy an early morning swim, before heading off for a round of putt-putt, and a visit to the ice creamery. My day is then wrapped up with a poolside barbeque and a few quiet beers whilst watching the kids swim, instead of the usual dancing and cocktails until dawn. Both scenarios are enjoyable; it's just a matter of deciding how you would like to spend your time and what parts of your life you would be happy and willing to change.

Another aspect of parenting worth considering, is whether you are prepared to share your life and your partner with another person, especially an extremely demanding little person who needs constant entertainment and has really different ideas of what fun is. I know a lot of people with children, and when I ask them out to do something, they usually respond with comments like, 'I would love to come, but Saturdays are crazy for us. Maybe we can stop in for an hour between Maddie's dance competition and Jackson's soccer match. I will have to let you know.'

If you have friends with children, this response may sound familiar. It shows that whilst parents determine most of what goes on in their day-to-day lives, they always make decisions also based on their children's needs. When trying to picture yourself as a parent, remember that your day won't stop at the close of business at five o'clock. And you will often need to either compromise or give up something you love in order to meet your child's needs.

Once you have explored your feelings about compromise and your future, you next need to examine the reasons you and your partner may want to start a family. Many of us have fond memories of childhood, family traditions, and lots of happy times being part of a family unit. The first twenty years of our lives are usually quite family oriented, so it is only natural for us to look at family life favourably. Those of us with fond memories want to recreate the positive aspects of our own childhood (and those who experienced more difficult childhoods will often want their children to enjoy what they missed out on), so it is easy to fantasise about a future filled with Easter eggs hunts, Sunday evening roasts, and long summer vacations by the beach. But parenting a child is so much more than that. It requires a lot of time and effort, and the ability to take the good times with the bad.

Regardless of your reasons for starting a family, it is undeniably gratifying to think that a part of you and your personal history will be passed on to future generations after you are gone. But before we get too far into this subject, let's explore in a little more detail that infamous 'biological clock' and the basic tradition of the family unit.

Chapter 2

Tick! Tock! Is That My Biological Clock?

It's only natural

Despite our iPods, broadband connections, and designer shoes, we are all just mammals with the primary purpose and mission in life to reproduce in order to ensure the continuation of the human race. By all accounts, we have been doing a pretty decent job of that so far.

Most women are born with an instinctual need to nurture and be nurtured, which makes us grow up believing that our transition into motherhood will be simple and natural. It is, after all, what Mother Nature intended.

When we seriously begin to dissect it, our desire to have a child should be no different to that of a lioness that each year goes into heat, gets pregnant, and delivers her cubs. The lioness follows what nature intended for her and does not question whether she wants a baby. It's pure instinct, as simple and uncomplicated as drinking from a stream when thirsty.

As human females, we are groomed to be parents and caregivers from a young age. Under the belief that we will one day start a family, adults introduce us to adult life early, and we practice being mummies by playing house and caring for our dollies. It's almost as if our purpose is already determined. Even back in caveman times, men hunted and gathered and women nurtured and protected. It seems so natural that it's hard to believe we all don't just wake up, have a strong feeling that having a baby is the right thing to do, and then follow that instinct. When we look at motherhood this way, it's no wonder that many of us believe there is something wrong with us when we have doubts about what Mother Nature intended.

From as early as the first time we see a pregnant woman, through to our teenage years when our bodies begin to develop, women have no doubt about what we are designed for. Whilst the boys are out playing sports and conquering the world, a girl will get her period, watch her breasts swell and spend the majority of her life trying not to get pregnant. She knows that she has been built to have a baby and that she has the incredible ability to create life. And in the past, growing up to become a wife and mother was the norm for girls.

But things are different now, and many of us are growing up to understand that there is more to life than having children: more options, more ways to live. Thus, we begin to question our instincts and the traditional—and often expected—path to parent-hood.

As time passes and a woman makes a life with her own traditions, goals, and routines, she may begin to consider whether she wants to change that life and make sacrifices to start a family. Some people may call this kind of thinking selfish, but I prefer to call it realistic.

It's what people do

If you look around, you will probably notice that just about everyone is becoming a parent, from your best friend to the girl at work to the hottest actor in Hollywood. And with all the hype, and women of every age and background trading in their purse-sized puppies for a pram and a belly bump, you certainly cannot be blamed for thinking, *well, if so and so is doing it, then why shouldn't I?*

In today's world of social networking and targeted advertising, we are constantly surrounded by outside influences like shared values, trends, and ideas that are extremely difficult to ignore when embraced by others. This physiological process is so common that there's even a name for it: internalisation.

When something is 'the norm', and everyone else around you is doing it, the decision-making process becomes even more difficult. Those external pressures and societal ideals can leave you confused about how *you* feel.

I can remember the astonished looks on people's faces when, even in 2006, I still did not own or carry a mobile phone. People would look at me as if I were out of my mind. How could I possibly live without a mobile phone? It was almost twenty-first-century blasphemy.

When you think about how opinionated people are about something so simple as owning a piece of technology, then you have to wonder what kind of chance you have when you question something as primal as family.

Most of us probably experienced some form of peer pressure in our school days. As adults, we should be free of that and aim to be our own person. It's not always easy, but you must push those powerful outside influences aside and do what is comfortable and reasonable for *you*. Because once you start thinking, *if everyone is doing it, it must be the right thing to do*, you will to start to doubt yourself and your convictions.

When is the best time?

It isn't just a decision about whether or not to have a child that keeps us up at night. Many women who are swaying towards the yes side wonder when the best time may be to have a child. Some of us hope that if we wait for the right time to present itself, then both the decision and the transition into motherhood will be easier.

However, what I have seen since becoming a mother is that there genuinely is no 'right time' to have a baby. This new addition to your life is going be a massive shock. And no specific preparation is going to help you be ready for the challenge of parenthood, no matter your age, fitness level, or financial situation. If you continuously delay the decision by waiting for the perfect time, the perfect job, the perfect home, and the perfect financial situation, you will end up trapped in the waiting game, never quite committing yourself one way or the other, and possibly leaving the decision until it's too late.

That said, there are certainly better and worse times to have a baby. If you are currently paying off three credit cards, going through a restructure at work, renovating your home, and finishing a degree, then right now may not be the best time to start a family. But, if your life is as normal as it's ever going to be, you feel both physically and mentally well, and have checked your financial status, then now is probably about as good a time as any.

I certainly didn't wake up one morning, evaluate my life, and think, *hey, this is the perfect time to have a baby!* For me, the decision was a long, drawn-out thought process. In the years preceding my final decision, there was always something going on or coming up in my life that would be time-consuming, stressful, or expensive. And every time we passed one obstacle and found some breathing space, there was always another one waiting on the horizon. In retrospect, no time would have been a 'good time'; there would have always been some situation to prompt us to delay the decision.

Now that I know that I could have done nothing to prepare myself for motherhood, and my transition into parenthood would have been the same now, or seven years ago, I sometimes wish we had started a family earlier. Not that we don't feel fit and capable as older parents, or that we worry about keeping up with the kids in the future, it's just that it would be have been nice to have been a little younger when our daughter entered her early adult years. But given my mental and physical state when I was twenty-six—

and despite the fact I had a stable job and a good home—I also know that I would not have been ready for motherhood then. In fact, missing out on that part of my youth may have led me to resent motherhood.

Life rarely turns out the way we want it to and will always be filled with challenges and surprises. You cannot plan for every contingency. But I honestly believe that you don't need everything to be perfect in order to be the perfect parent. You just need your heart in the right place, and your baby will be perfect regardless. So, instead of worrying about the 'right time', read this book, talk with your partner, and do some serious soul searching. Hopefully, by the time you have reached the end of my journey, the answer will have come to you.

And don't be surprised if you change your mind two or three times during the process. It is perfectly normal and does not mean that you are an indecisive person. In fact, it just proves you have the emotional maturity needed to allow yourself time to go through a range of emotions and feelings, which can only help you make your decision from a position of confidence.

Chapter 3

Outside Pressures and Regrets

People in general both choose to and want to live as part of a community. The majority of us are brought up in a family unit that may comprise aunts, uncles, cousins, and grandparents, and may even be part of a larger cultural or religious group. We are brought up to value the opinions of those close to us and with the desire to please the ones we love. Whilst being part of a large community offers benefits such as security, support, and companionship, it can also mean loss of privacy and autonomy in our personal lives, especially when it comes to private life decisions. To make others happy, we are sometimes expected, or simply choose, to do things we would not otherwise want to do. Such sacrifices are often considered 'compromises' and generally, a person who compromises and gives to others without complaint or concern for their own feelings is looked upon as noble.

Whilst selflessly giving to others without the expectation of anything in return is a highly desirable and admirable personal attribute, when it comes to the motherhood question, it can also be your downfall. You may feel obligated to bend to outside pressure, or be influenced or even bullied into making a decision that should be exclusively yours. In this case, it is paramount to remember that you do not need to prove your womanhood to anyone. No matter what, motherhood is your choice!

Almost anyone with a womb can have a baby, but not everyone is born to be a good parent, nor is everyone born with the desire to be one. Regardless of what other people or socialisation may lead you to believe, you are not selfish if you decide that motherhood is not the right choice for you. Motherhood is not your job by default. It has been and always will be your choice, and you alone must examine your own reasons for wanting or not wanting a baby.

For many people, and women, in particular, there can be a steady stream of external pressure to reproduce, whether from family and friends or from society, in general. Whilst this pressure can sometimes be overwhelming and weigh down your convictions, you must stand guard and keep your ground. You must NEVER let outside pressure influence a decision of this magnitude.

Now let's take a closer look at some of the places this pressure may come from.

Outside Pressures

My religion encourages it

For active members of a church or religious organisation, the decision not to have children may be in direct contrast to the teachings of your religion, and may be in direct conflict with the way you have been raised. This conflict with your religious values may leave you feeling guilty about 'secretly betraying' your family, pastor or religious leader, and faith community.

Considering that your parents may not be happy with your decision and that you may experience some backlash from your religious community, you may find it difficult to go against the grain. In this case, however, you only have two options: deny your own wishes and conform to other people's beliefs and convictions, or be brave and do what is best for you and your partner.

If religion is a fundamental part of your life, it is vital that you discuss the family issue with your pastor or church leader before marriage. With the guidance of an understanding minister, you will be able to focus on understanding what a successful marriage, with or without children, actually requires: compatibility, friendship, compromise, and the ability to maintain open and honest communication.

Then you will need to deal with the reactions of your family members who may not understand your reservations about parenthood and, even more dire, your decision not to have children. You will need to explain how you feel, and assure them that your decision does not change your beliefs, and that you are still the same person with the same values, morals, and love for your family and faith. Also, let them know that they raised you right, that you love them, and that you respect their opinions. Hopefully, they will understand that you know what makes you happy, and will trust you to make the right decision for *you*.

Should your family or religious community not understand your situation, you will need to remain strong in your convictions. Remember that whilst your morals, beliefs and behaviour complement and are a part of your faith, they do not define you as a person. Having a baby only to conform to your spiritual values or pressure from your church group or family may seem easier at the time, but it may not be enough in itself to make you a happy wife and mother.

On a personal level, deciding not to have a child will not change how you think about or practice your religion or interact with your community. We may have been created to be biologically capable of having children, but we are also biologically designed to be strong, independent women with the ability to make decisions about the paths our lives take. No matter how hard a decision may seem, you must remember to trust in yourself.

If your and your partner's backgrounds are vastly different, then this is a topic that should be brought up early in a relationship, so everyone has a chance to have his or her beliefs given equal consideration, whether they are from an ethnic, cultural, or religious point of view. And the good news is, that once you have reached an amicable agreement, and are both on the same page; you will at least have each other for moral and emotional support when it comes time to discuss your feelings with family and friends.

Mum wants grandkids

After a couple marries, family members will often overwhelm them with questions about when they will start having babies. For many parents, it is a long-held dream and even expectation that their own children will provide them with grandchildren. Whilst most of us love our parents and want to make them happy, no couple should allow themselves to be pressured into having children under any circumstances. Having a baby is a monumental commitment, and if you and your partner are not utterly convinced that you are ready for a family, then it is likely that you are indeed not ready yet.

If you do find yourself receiving pressure from your parents to start a family, you need to take action by taking them aside and telling them how you both feel. Let them know that whilst you appreciate their desire to have grandchildren, you need to live your life the way you want to, and for now that means being child-free. But assure them that if and when children join the equation, they will be the first to know.

He wants to be a dad

Contrary to popular belief, it isn't always women who are nagging their husbands to start a family sooner rather than later. In some cases, it is the man who wants to become a daddy tomorrow, whilst his wife doesn't feel ready yet, if at all.

As a woman, it may seem strange not to feel clucky when your partner is raring to go, but if you are in this situation, you need to stop doubting yourself, and know that this situation is not unusual. It is actually healthy and quite common for couples to be at different stages in their lives, and thus be ready to become parents at different times.

A woman in this situation may feel pressure from her partner and maybe even his parents, and may feel responsible for giving him the child he wants. Some women may even begin to think along the lines, *well, I did marry him. It is my wifely duty. Isn't it?*

The answer to this question is unequivocally no! The only reason you should ever consider having a baby is because you want one. Despite your partner's desires, you are the one who will have to give up your body to carry a baby for nine months, and it will be you who will have to take on the primary responsibility for feeding and caring for the child during its early days.

Even in today's modern world where the traditional domestic roles are becoming more evenly balanced, in most cases, it is still the woman who takes on the majority of the burden of raising a child—and this is true even if she works or has other commitments that take up a lot of her time and energy, such as caring for an elderly parent or assisting in the community.

Ideally, this is something that should be discussed before you commit to marriage or a lifetime relationship. But if you and your partner clearly have opposing life goals and cannot come to a compromise then you need to seriously discuss the future of your relationship and whether you do have a future together. Perhaps, for some this may mean saying goodbye and letting your partner go and allow them to start a family with someone else, before your relationship crumbles by default.

It's a family tradition

Many people come from a tradition of large families, particularly in certain cultures. Age-old family traditions may not only en-courage a large number of children, but also expect that the family lineage be honoured through the naming of children after family members.

Most of us feel strong family ties, so a woman can often feel tre-mendous pressure to succumb to her family's dream of a dozen grandchildren gathered around the old oak dining table. If you come from a traditional family that expects you to carry on the family name, then many members of your extended family may struggle with the idea that you might only have one or two chil-dren or even none at all.

In this case, the best course of action is to tackle the subject head on. Talking honestly with each family member to let each one know how you feel may buy you some time but be warned that even this approach may not achieve results. You may still find that no matter how well you explain yourself, certain family members will never be satisfied with your decision and may never be able to let the matter go. Be strong. Hopefully with time, your family will learn to trust your judgement and find a way to live with it. And think of all the time and energy you will have to be a fantastic aunt to your beloved nieces and nephews.

People just keep asking me

No one asks you about having kids when you are twenty-three. But once you reach thirty and beyond, people become very interested in when you are going to start a family and why you haven't started one before now. I cannot count the times people asked me when I was going to have children. And I was always amused by the shock on people's faces when they learned that Brad and I had been together for years, were in our mid-thirties, and still didn't have kids. Whilst it didn't seem strange to us, many people believe that people of a certain age in a committed relationship will naturally have children.

As a couple, we noticed that people's concerns grew stronger as we grew older. It seemed that everyone wanted to express their concerns about what would happen to us if we didn't hurry up and get going. I don't think it ever occurred to any of them that we might not have cared if we missed out, or that we might have no intention of having a family at all.

Unfortunately, it can be difficult to put an end to the unsolicited advice of well-meaning people, so the best thing to do is smile and take it on the chin. And on those days when you are not in the mood to accommodate people, tell them about the exciting weekend you have planned. Sometimes distracting people from the issue and focusing on how great your life is at the moment is enough to make them drop the subject.

In summary

There are many wonderful reasons to have children, and children undoubtedly add happiness and joy to our lives. However, it is important for prospective parents to understand and evaluate their own motivations for having children. If you decide to have a baby for one or more of the above reasons, it is probably a good idea to wait until you have further explored your own reasons so you can be confident you have reached a conclusion on your own. Remember, there is nothing wrong with not wanting to have a baby or with taking more time to think about it. Don't let other people's impatience waive your resolve.

Regrets

Oh, regrets! One of the annoying parts of becoming both older and wiser is that you have the ability to look back on past decisions with clear and knowing eyes—and to realise that some of your decisions may not have been in your best interest. But the past is the past, and rather than waste time wondering *what if?* we just have to accept what has come before, learn from it, and move on.

When it comes to having kids, though, couples are often plagued with doubt and tormented by two possible scenarios:

What if I have a baby and then regret it?

What if I don't have a baby, and then I regret it when it's too late to change my mind?

What if I regret having a baby?

You may be surprised to know that, given the choice again, some mothers would not have had a baby. Not that they regret having the children they have now, or love them any less, but what these women have come to realise is that motherhood asks for more than they may have been prepared to give, and entails sacrifices they were not ready for or not willing to make. When you are already happy in your current life, it is normal to wonder whether the family lifestyle and the changes it will bring will allow you to continue to be happy, and if you will indeed enjoy being a parent at all.

When it comes to children, many of us truly believe that we have some idea as to what to expect and use our past experience—whether it be from babysitting or helping raise a younger sibling—as a basis for understanding how we feel about having a family. But despite the background and experience, I would say that most new parents are genuinely surprised at how drastically parenthood affects every single aspect of their lives.

Often women who are highly organised and successful in both their home and work lives think that reading the books, attending all the classes, and making sure their support mechanisms are in place will mean an easier transition into motherhood. But, what can happen is that things don't go according to plan when the big day arrives, and instead of the perfect picture of motherhood and gurgling babies they had envisioned, they are instead left entirely overwhelmed, stressed, and unhappy. Their feelings, of not being in control, can mean their transition into motherhood is nothing short of an absolute disaster. But often once the hard years of infancy are gone and their lives start feeling more normal, they begin to experience the joy they had hoped motherhood would bring.

Of course, there will always be some mothers who, whilst they love their children and have a life full of happy memories, would still choose not to become mothers if given the choice again. In retrospect, they realise that they would have been just as happy had they chosen a child-free life.

Unfortunately, no one can predict the future. And like most significant life decisions, such as moving to another state or country, changing careers, or getting married, you will need to weigh the potential pros and cons and assess the risks. It is also important to make sure you are mentally ready for the challenge ahead and fully understand the true nature of parenting.

Society often leads us to believe that when your child is born, you will inherently know what you need to do, have the skills and knowledge to raise your child properly, and love doing it. It seems we are seldom told about the downside—the doubts, the lack of confidence, and the tears that flow when you are a new parent. And they definitely don't tell you about the times that you will love, but not actually like, your child.

I have met and spoken to hundreds of mums, of which only two have confided to me that they have not transcended into what they would class as "the motherly type," and have sometimes wondered if they made the right decision. But despite their feelings, both of these women are terrific mothers and neither would ever give their children back!

The truth is that most of us parents do have days when we wish we could go back and enjoy a few days of our past lives (often this wishing would take place around 3 o'clock in the morning) but I have yet to meet anyone who actually regrets having children. So how does this help you? Is there a chance you could regret having a baby? If you don't head down this path with your eyes and heart wide open, then yes, you may experience some feelings of regret. But if you feel as ready as you will ever be, have a strong support system, and are in a happy and stable relationship, then there is certainly no reason why you can't join the millions of other women around the world that don't just do it once, but enjoy it enough to do it two or three times, or even more.

And if worse comes to worst, once you are in the "Mother's Club" you are allowed to whinge or cry into your champagne glass whenever you feel like it, and no one will ever begrudge you for it. In fact, your girlfriends may just join in.

Will I regret NOT having a baby?

Like many of you, I raced through the last few decades so busy having a good time that I thought the ticking sound I occasionally heard was my girlfriend's porcelain nails tapping on the bar whilst we waited for our Friday afternoon mudslides. And to this day I can distinctly remember the moment when this belief was shattered.

I was on my lunch break filling out a form. After completing the usual opening questions, I reached the part pertaining to age. On autopilot, I placed my pen in the box labelled twenty-six to thirty-four and was about to complete my tick when I suddenly realised that I was no longer in that category. *Oh my God! I'm not twenty-seven! I don't get to tick this box. I have to tick the box for old people, the one for thirty-five to forty-nine-year-olds.* I was stunned. In those few moments as my pen hovered over the page I became aware that I was in the post office and not at the hottest new bar in town. I took a sharp breath as the realisation hit me. *That annoying ticking isn't Karen's nails at all! It's my biological clock!*

For a split second, my heart fluttered and I panicked. Hadn't I just read somewhere that your eggs begin to dry up at around thirty-five? Yes, it was in that gossip magazine I had flicked through the week before at the hairdresser whilst having my roots done. My heart fluttered again. Then, two seconds later, to my overwhelming relief, I recalled another article in the same magazine about a sixty-year-old woman giving birth in Peru.

I relaxed even further as I remembered all the women in Hollywood having twins in their forties. *And I'm nowhere near forty yet. Plus I eat organic food and do Pilates three times a week. What on earth am I worrying about?* Relieved that the problem had been solved—or at least put on hold—I happily finished filling out my form, submitted it and ran back to work. By the time the executive meeting started an hour later, I had forgotten all about it.

Whilst at the time this revelation came as a shock, it did make me realise that one of the main reasons that thoughts of family flit in and out of our minds so quickly is that many of us are stuck in a place where we just cannot choose. It is such a monumental decision that most of us don't take the time or energy to sit down and have a truly good think about it.

Unfortunately for all of us, this decision will never be black and white. If it were as easy as figuring out if you can afford a baby, you could simply work out the sums, make a budget, and end up with a straightforward answer. But how can anyone possibly know if they are going to regret something? How can we possibly know how we are going to feel about something twenty years from now?

It's not like regretting that you didn't go backpacking after high school, because Italy will always be there. This is something that actually has a scientifically proven use-by date attached to it. And for a generation of women that typically can have everything they have ever wanted, this finality scares and confuses us equally.

The other problem is the distinct lack of people around to ask for advice about this issue. By now, your best girlfriends have either already had children or are in the same boat as you. The other respected and influential women in your life, like your mother, aunties, and grandmothers, all come from an age where childrearing was the norm. That is why this question is so much harder for our generation to answer, as we truly are the pioneers of "To mum or not to mum?"

Thirty years from now, women will actually have a broader range of information available to them. Future generations will live in an age of one-child families and neighbourhoods no longer overflowing with children, which may lead them to have different views on children and families than we do now. Their decision will definitely be easier thanks to a larger pool of women to talk to, women who will be able to provide some insight as to whether the decision not to have children had been right for them. Whilst the choice will always need to be made carefully, women of the future will at least have some resources and experiences to help them shape their own decisions.

But what about those of us in the here and now? How do you know what you may or may not regret? You don't. You can only make the best decision possible for you and your circumstances, go in with your eyes open, and remember that you won't know what you'll regret until it is too late to change your mind.

Will I regret not being a grandparent?

I imagine most of us have thought about what our lives might be like when we get older and our days are no longer planned out for us. Many have fantasised about the pitter-patter of tiny feet, and of spending our free time playing in parks, visiting the zoo, and spoiling our grandchildren thoroughly rotten in our retirement.

I have always loved the idea of being a grandmother and have often daydreamed about replicating my magical memories of warm afternoons reading stories on my grandmother Elizabeth's knee, and getting thoroughly soaked with bubbles as my grandad and I washed his treasured old car and sang nursery rhymes.

But as fond as I was of this future me, I never saw myself having children just to make those dreams a reality. Secretly I had hoped that by some miracle I could get my treasured grandchildren without actually having to go to all the trouble of raising a family of my own. As time went by, I realised that if I honestly did want to have grandchildren one day, then I would actually have to bite the bullet and start a family. The more I thought about it, the more I thought that I would be sad if I missed out on all the wonderful things that come with having family around later in life. Was I prepared to forgo family milestones like helping to plan weddings, and attending graduations, talent quests, and Christmas pageants? Or spending hours wandering around museums or playing in water parks, with nothing else to do but lavish love and attention on my family, and those lovely little grandchildren of mine?

There can never be a clear answer to whether *you* will regret having or not having children. All you can do for now is look into your heart, evaluate who you are and what makes you truly happy, and then listen to that gut instinct of yours.

Chapter 4

Who Else Will Be on this Journey?

Parenthood is an epic journey, a trip certainly made easier if you have a travelling buddy or two. Whilst gone are the days when a child was "raised by a village", it is still beneficial to think about who will be joining you on this lifelong adventure, and where you can get support and guidance along the way. Although a supportive partner will certainly make a difference on a day-to-day basis, whether you can readily rely on support from outside the family home can make an enormous difference in your life as a whole.

Do I have the right partner?

Before you have a child with someone, take stock of that person's behaviour, character, and lifestyle. You may be madly in love with your city-hopping, rock-and-roll boyfriend now, but if you are seriously considering joining the ranks of motherhood, you will need to stop and evaluate whether his lifestyle and views on commitment, compromise, and sacrifice are conducive to settling down and having a family.

And it isn't just the wild and carefree boyfriends we need to be thinking about here; even a somewhat settled partner may be showing signs that he is not ready for the responsibility of parent-hood simply by sitting back and letting you run around looking after his every need, or by putting everything else before the relationship. One simple way to determine if your partner has the capacity to be flexible in a family situation is to consider whether, on short notice, he would be prepared to give up a regular catch-up with the boys in order to come along and give you moral support at a family or work function. How much commitment he shows for your relationship now could have a direct bearing on his readiness to start a family later on.

Conversely, a partner who may seem ready may in fact not be. If your partner is considering furthering his education by going back to school or simply has a successful and demanding career that takes up most of his time and energy, he may not be around to give you the support you need, leaving you to care for the baby on your own most of the time. If your partner is career-focused, yet you are sure he is the one for you, then you will have to factor this into your decision.

Regardless of the type of partner you have, if you are serious about having a child then you will need to look long and hard at your life and your relationships, both as they are now and how they may be in the future. If you are already married, then hopefully you have considered your life plans and goals together before the wedding, and know how you both feel about having children. If you are in a newish relationship, or have been living in a de-facto relationship for a long time, you may not have sat down and really discussed the subject so this is something you definitely need to do before taking the next steps.

Here are some possible questions to consider when speaking with your partner about possible parenthood:

Does my partner have the right temperament to be a parent?

Is our relationship rock solid, or do we still have some underlying issues to sort out?

Does my partner want to have children when I do? Or even at all?

Are we able to provide the child a safe and happy home, with no external pressures such as personal afflictions or excessive debts?

Is our home free of constant tension and arguments?

Are my partner and I really ready to settle down?

I know that some of these questions are tough and may be difficult to answer; however, it is vital that you take the time to think about and accept the answers. Remember, once your child is born, you will be linked to this person and their family for the rest of your and your child's life—even if your marriage or relationship does not work out.

Same-sex couples

A few decades ago, being single or gay usually meant giving up any hope of becoming a parent. But things have changed, and society is finally realising that *everyone* has a maternal clock. Unfortunately, although it is becoming more common for same-sex couples to follow their dream of becoming parents, they often must face more challenges than a traditional couple, which only makes their choice that much more difficult.

Whilst same-sex couples will have the usual doubts and fears that any potential parent has to contend with, they may also have to deal with additional issues, such as finding a suitable egg or sperm donor, deciding who will carry their child, and choosing who will take on the role of primary caregiver. Additional headaches may not stop there, since many couples will face ongoing issues during their child-raising years, including dealing with the emotional turmoil of having their children teased at school, or having to cope with certain people not agreeing with their lifestyle choices. They will probably also need to be even more vigilant than the average parent to help ensure their children are not discriminated against and receive the same opportunities as others. It is a shame that issues like these even need to be considered, but if we are to be realistic, we have to acknowledge that we live in a world in which prejudice and discrimination are a part of our everyday lives. How comfortable your children will feel at school will depend on how open you and your kids are about your family structure, and how much support you receive from those around you. You probably already realise there will be people who will disagree with your decision. However, if you decide to start a family, then you will need to accept that other people are just as entitled to their opinion as you are to yours.

If you come from a large and diverse family, then your children will have no problems getting the balanced life experience they need. Just because your child has two mummies or two daddies doesn't also mean that your child, like all other children, won't also have four aunties, three uncles, four grandparents, and a dozen or more cousins to provide the balance they need. If you don't have a large family or your family do not live in your proximity then perhaps you might find close friends who can fill those roles as substitute aunts and uncles etc.?

If you have a strong support system, and have the strength of character to deal with the unsolicited opinions of others, then you simply need to make this decision the same way any other couple does: by assessing if you are physically, emotionally, and financially ready to have a child.

Going it alone

Statistics show that at least half of all children will be raised solely by one parent at some point in their lives, whether due to death, divorce, separation, or because the single parent had decided to go it alone in the first place. It is becoming exceedingly more common for single women to take baby-making matters into their own hands, particularly in the case of highly educated and professional women who have dedicated their lives to building a career rather than focusing on their personal lives.

Even many single men are now adding their voices to the mix, wondering how they can satisfy their hopes of becoming a father if they don't find the right woman to marry. Men in record numbers are admitting that they have serious concerns about missing out on fatherhood, and don't want to take the chance of not meeting the right partner in time. Some men, including even a few well-known celebrities, have acted upon these fears by exploring options such as surrogacy and adoption as ways to fulfil their dream of becoming a parent.

Whilst being a single parent is not always ideal—in fact, some people consider it selfish or wrong in some way—for many, single parenthood may be the only option to experience the joy of family life.

If you are considering entering into parenthood alone, it is important that, along with all the usual questions a potential parent must ask herself, you also take into account the added stresses and pressures that will come with single parenthood.

Whether you want to go it alone out of choice or because other factors have directed your decision, remember that millions of children have been raised by single parents, and most of them have turned out just fine.

Who else can help me during pregnancy and beyond?

Having a support system is one of *the* most essential things during pregnancy and the early months of motherhood and is one of *the* things that will determine how well you handle, and how much you enjoy, the early days of being a mum.

When evaluating your potential support system, start by considering the following questions:

Once pregnant, will your spouse or another family member be available to attend appointments with you?

Is anyone available to help you out around the house when you are tired or too sick to do anything?

Once the baby is home, will your partner be able to take time off work to help you both settle in?

Do you have family or friends that can drop by and help with housework and cooking meals, or simply give you an occasional time out when you just need a break?

If you are lucky, your or your partner's family lives close by, or you have a tonne of friends willing to help out during the tough times. Remember, though, that whilst you may receive assistance in the beginning, the reality is that things often change as the newness wears off. Both friends and family necessarily get busy with their own lives and children, so don't expect the new-baby support system to be a permanent fixture. Becoming a mum means always being on-call no matter how many happy helpers you have.

Chapter 5

Having Doubts – Mind, Body & Spirit

Emotional concerns

When debating the baby question, couples often focus on their physical health and forget all about the emotional aspects of having a baby. But how emotionally prepared you both are will definitely affect how well you manage, and how much you enjoy, being parents. On this journey, you want to be as ready in your head as you are in your heart.

Life as a new parent is tough. You will need to learn to tolerate the constant demands of a child, as well as the strong feelings that a child can evoke, such as frustration, incompetence, and vulnerability. Many women, no matter how well prepared, are shocked at how different their lives are once their baby arrives, and are genuinely surprised at how many emotions and stresses a young child can provoke.

There is a significant adjustment period in the early days of motherhood, and the strong sense of responsibility and selflessness that a new baby requires can be overwhelming for many women. As enjoyable as parenting is, it can be quite daunting to have someone else's entire existence and daily happiness resting solely upon your shoulders. Understanding where you are now both emotionally and mentally, as well as being prepared to accept the bad with the good, is one of the first steps in determining if you are ready for motherhood.

You have probably asked yourself the same questions about your suitability and readiness for motherhood that most women have asked themselves at some point. Let's look at some of these common questions in more detail.

Am I too young?

Everyone likes to talk about the right age to start a family, but there really is no magic age. I know some pretty switched-on twenty-one-year-olds who would already make fantastic parents, as well as some still very young and naïve forty-year-olds who are definitely not ready to settle down and have a family. Every person is different and at very different stages of emotional maturity, so the ideal time to start a family will vary depending on the individual.

In your twenties, you are often focused on your career and simply enjoying life on a day-to-day basis. Having children is usually just a vague idea to consider later on down the track after you have lived a little. You figure that you will consider your options carefully when the time is right.

Some young women, on the other hand, do want to start a family earlier in life, and may wonder if they are too young. Of course, women are physically capable of having children from a young age, but the age at which a woman actually becomes a mother can matter a great deal. Without a doubt, there is a real emotional and psychological maturity that comes with age and life experience that can help make motherhood less stressful and more enjoyable, not to mention the financial and physical security that usually accompanies age.

Whilst there are lots of positives to waiting to start a family, there are also many benefits of being a younger parent, such as having a safer and less physically demanding pregnancy, having the energy to keep up with a young child, and being a younger and more active grandparent. Lots of young women have made excellent mothers. But if you are wondering whether you are too young, that doubt may be a clue for you to wait until you feel less uncertain and more ready to take on such a big challenge. You want to get the timing right so that you can truly enjoy parenting, rather than risk becoming resentful of the time that motherhood takes from other areas of your life. Often just realising that motherhood can be difficult and demanding can help you choose when the time is right for you.

Am I too old?

When I was in primary school, I can only remember two kids in my year whose parents were older than the average parents I knew, and by older, I mean late thirties to forties. Almost all of our parents were in their late twenties, and for our generation, young parents were the norm. I can even picture the look on James' and Julie's faces when every afternoon their parents would arrive and some kid would laugh and yell, "Hey, look, your grandparents are here." Looking back, I realise that whilst this teasing was cruel, it was also a sign of the times.

Fast forward twenty years and times have certainly changed. Now the number of babies born to women aged forty and over is greater than the number of births to teenagers. Even the way we grow into adulthood has changed, with many children now staying with their parents until they finish university or simply choosing to hang around home until they are well into their twenties. For this new generation, starting a family is the last thing on their minds. When you add to this the fact that many couples are delaying having children until much later in life, you can easily see why thirty-five has become the new twenty-five.

Some women wonder if they will look stupid or be the oldest mother at antenatal classes and school events if they choose to have a child later in life. But Australian Bureau of Statistics figures show that at least half of all babies are now born to mothers over the age of thirty, and many of these are to women in their late thirties and early forties.

As I walked into my first antenatal class I did wonder how I would look next to all the young mums-to-be, but ended up being pleasantly surprised to find that most of the other couples were in our age group or older, and therefore we all had lots in common and felt entirely comfortable. Being a first-time mum at thirty-six worked well for me, but whilst having children later in life is commonplace these days, you do need to remember that delaying children does mean an increase in certain risks. As this subject is pretty close to my heart, I have expanded on it in more detail later on.

Emotional maturity

Being solely responsible for the well being of another human being is nothing short of overwhelming! Realising that you have to be entirely selfless, put someone else's needs before your own, and be able to love that person unconditionally—no matter what they do, how hard it gets, or how angry they make you feel—can lead many women to wonder if they may be taking on a job that they might not be able nor really want to do.

Emotional maturity has nothing to do with age; rather, it is some-thing gained only through life experience, and is more about the type of person you are and how well you deal with responsibility than how many years you have lived. Someone who has lived a full life, dealt with hardships, and had to take on responsibility from a young age may be better equipped to deal with the pressures of motherhood than someone ten years older who has lived an easier and more sheltered life.

When considering if you are emotionally ready to have a child, think about how you live your life now, how you feel about re-sponsibility and compromise, and how you feel when things don't go your way. Then ask yourself some questions:

Are you always late?

Do you change jobs every few months?

Do you move so often that your mother has an address book exclusively for you?

Do you still consider Friday as party night after a hectic work week?

Do your future fantasies include backpacking around Europe or saving up for a new designer dress?

If you answered yes to any of those questions, it may be an indication that you need to live life a little more before you are emotionally and mentally ready to provide the stability and commitment a child needs. That doesn't mean you will never be a mother or a terrific parent; it just suggests that the time may not be quite right for you now.

Do I really know what I want?

Before becoming a mother, I spent many years looking into myself trying to determine what I actually wanted out of life and whether motherhood would make me happy. People often say that nobody knows you more than you know yourself, but when it came to the baby decision, I didn't feel like I knew myself very well at all, particularly since I couldn't even make a decision about something that is supposed to be the most natural part of being a woman.

Big life changes aren't easy, so when making such a huge decision it's often helpful to break the problem down into smaller, more manageable pieces. Instead of asking yourself, *do I want to have a baby?* try visualising yourself as a mother and think about how you would handle it. Could you learn to budget, compromise, and live with a certain amount of chaos? Would you be willing and able to share your life and dedicate yourself wholly to the happiness and well-being of another human being?

Also think about the qualities you need to be a good parent such as patience, forgiveness, and selflessness, and determine whether you have these traits or the ability to learn them. Consider whether you actually like children: whether you enjoy talking to them, listening to their ideas, playing their games and getting involved in activities they enjoy. Then try to imagine yourself holding both a screaming and colicky infant, then a gurgling six-month-old. Attempt to visualise all aspects of parenting, not just the good parts! Remember that along with the fun and laughter a child will bring, you will also have to deal with nightmares, bullying, and the never-ending sagas that inevitably come with raising a child.

Making this decision is not easy, but if you take the time to consider all of these questions, look into your heart and find the right answers, then you may find that you do know yourself better than you imagined and that you do have what it takes to become a mother.

Will I lose myself?

Motherhood is often a thankless twenty-four hour a day job, so it's quite common to wonder if you will lose your own identity in the act of becoming a mother. Will you still be seen as the intelligent, outgoing, and sophisticated woman you are today, or instead be seen only as "little Billy's mother"? Will people suddenly stop asking your opinion on politics and world events, and instead look for you only when someone gets chewing gum stuck in their hair?

The thought of losing one's identity is frightening, and I admit that this was one of my greatest fears. At first I thought I was just resisting change, but once I became pregnant, some of those fears became a reality. Although I was still the same person on the inside, I was treated differently as soon as people realised I was expecting. Instead of asking me if I had seen a good movie or read a good book lately, people would see my tell-tale bump and fire off the same old predictable series of questions: *When are you due? Do you know if it is a boy or girl? Are you going to breastfeed?* Even my friends seemed to forget who I was, asking about my choice of names rather than the weekend's NRL game.

These changes were a little annoying at first, but when I thought about it, my pregnancy *was* an important part of my life, and it was nice to tell others about the impending birth of my child. It was only later that I began to find it a little frustrating. I knew that my pregnancy didn't define who I was, but others didn't seem to get that. Eventually, I got to the point where I just wanted people to treat me like a normal adult, not just a woman with a bump. I wanted the old me back.

Over time and as my pregnancy drew to an end, I started to hope that things might change once my daughter arrived. But that was not meant to be; instead I found that the simple act of having a baby meant that I was no longer seen as a single person, now I was a mother plus baby, or a family. Instead of their hands reaching out to my belly, their eyes would go straight to the pram and a new standard line of questions began: *Is she teething yet? Are you getting much sleep?* Again, whilst it was lovely to talk about my child and have a whinge about the lack of sleep, I craved adult conversation, mainly because I, like most new mums, had been locked up in the house all day with only the bub for company.

Of course, I can't assign the full blame to outsiders for contributing to my loss of self because my darling new baby had a lot to do with it too. From the day I brought my daughter home life as I knew it changed. No longer did I have the time or ability to do a lot of the things that I used to love. I could no longer just drop into the cinema to check out the latest blockbuster, and I certainly wouldn't be popping down to the beach for a quick dip with a newborn. I had to accept that most of my hobbies and interests would have to be put on hold.

During the hectic first years, the loss of freedom was hard to deal with, and there were certainly times when I felt like I had lost my identity. Even now that I am comfortable in family life, there are days when I cannot even remember who I used to be, days when I mourn my old life and the things I once took for granted. But whilst I admit I have lost a little bit of myself—okay, then, a big chunk of myself!—I have also gained some new parts in exchange. There is nothing like a baby to open up new feelings and allow you to realise that there is a lot more to you and your capabilities than you ever imagined. One of the things I have enjoyed most about becoming a mother is seeing the world through someone else's eyes. My daughter has allowed me to take time out of my busy schedule to decide what I want out of life, and what I want for my family. I think I finally understand and appreciate the term "work-life balance".

Remember, although you may have said goodbye to some hobbies for now, parenthood opens the doors to new interests and opportunities you may not have considered before. For example, if I hadn't been looking for an opportunity to spend more time with my daughter and make a better life for her, I probably never would have taken the time nor had the courage to pursue my lifelong dream of writing. This book would never have been conceived, and I would not have become the founder of a successful parenting website.

So, whilst you will lose some of your old self, you may also get a new and improved you too. And hey, your children won't be young forever.

Can I do it all?

Thanks to women's lib, we are no longer required to walk in the footsteps of Mrs Beaver and just stay home, care for the children, and cook the Sunday roast. Today's woman is expected to be a loving mother and wife, run a household, and hold down a job, all whilst still finding time to go to the gym, blow dry her hair, and keep herself looking fabulous.

We have also said goodbye to the days of the stereotypical stay-at-home mum—you know, the daggy type who would drop off the kids wearing her tracksuit pants and fuzzy slippers. Now, stay-at-home mothers are supposed to be glamorous "yummy mummies" who effortlessly care for their home and family whilst happily contributing to society and the community in their spare time. Nowadays she will run her household like clockwork, be the treasurer for the Girl Scouts, volunteer at the school canteen, and coordinate the local scrapbooking club. And of course none of these jobs will affect her ability to be a great best friend and daughter to those closest to her.

When you take into consideration all these expectations and the fact that most child-free couples already feel like their lives are filled to the brim, it is hard not to feel frightened and wonder if you will be able to do it all, particularly if you already feel time poor.

Having always known that mothers were the first up and the last to bed, before becoming one myself, I wondered how I would possibly fit a child into my life and still get everything done. What I have discovered is that I just don't get everything done. The sacrifices and compromises don't stop at giving up my Friday night cocktails with the girls, but rather they cover other aspects of my life, like having the perfect tidy home and being the super-organised and perfectly groomed woman I had once been.

Yes, I had to concede that I no longer have control over everything and that some things just don't happen when and how I want them to. I had to accept that things aren't always going to go my way and that I am not always going to get what I want. These were difficult adjustments to make, especially after years of running my life and my home the way I wanted to. Since becoming a parent, I have necessarily learnt that I have to let some things go and accept that everything isn't always going to be perfect.

And whilst I am learning to appreciate my natural hair colour and accept that sometimes we will have toasted sandwiches for dinner and leave the beds unmade, it is not all smiles. Sometimes it is really hard to believe that this is how my life is now. Before becoming a mother, I never realised how hard it is to try to do it all, and just how difficult it is to juggle both roles. I would often end up in tears when the old organised me had to give in to the disorganised frustrations of living with a young child.

With my maternity leave long gone, I am now trying desperately to adjust to my new life as a working mother. The fears I once had about how I would do everything whilst holding down a job are now a reality as I live every day in a haze of modern family life. On most days, the idea of actively contributing to the corporate world after being up half the night with a sick child and spending two hours in traffic seems almost impossible. But what I have found to be the hardest part about being a mother is realising that six o'clock doesn't mean a bath and a glass of wine; it means the beginning of the second shift of the dinner, bath, and bedtime routine. And it doesn't seem to matter how hard I work or how organised I am, most nights see me sitting down, not too many hours shy of midnight, wondering how on earth I will do it again tomorrow.

My weekends are now a juggling act of parks, shopping centres, and racing to see how much housework and online banking I can do during the midday nap. And in between all the extra jobs I now have, I still need to find the time, energy, and enthusiasm to amuse and entertain a bored and energetic toddler and a some-what neglected husband. This frantic pace leaves little to no time for hobbies, exercise, grooming, or "me" time. And more often than not the house cleaning gets neglected.

With my days and nights now a blur of activity, I have accepted that whilst I may be getting by, I am never going to be one of those super-efficient, glamorous, yummy mummies I mentioned earlier. I will probably never be able to do it all. Every day I have to try to change my perception of normal, but ultimately, I suppose that as long as we have food on the table and clean clothes on our backs, and still find time to relax and laugh together as a family, then that will have to be enough for now. I am sure there will be plenty of time in retirement to clean out the linen cupboards and sort out the family photo albums—as long as the kids don't rope me into babysitting the grandchildren to save on childcare costs.

Will I be able to cope?

Whilst having a baby will bring you joy and fill you with a love that you have never experienced before, it is at the same time both challenging and exhausting.

I truly believe that there just isn't enough information out there that explains to women just how stressful having a baby can be. Sometimes people fantasise about what having children will be like, so when the time comes they are not at all prepared for the toll it can take on both them and their relationships. Raising a child is not easy; in fact, it is often quite hard, and at times nothing short of total chaos. Having a strong and loving relationship with your partner, one in which you can openly communicate with each other, can certainly help you cope with motherhood. As parents, you will need an endless supply of love and forgiveness for each other, so that when times do get tough you can be each other's rock and provide the physical and emotional support the other person needs.

When we use a term like "being able to cope", it is usually in a very general sense in that if we will be able to "cope" with a child, it means all the time, no matter what. Whilst you do need a certain strength of character to deal with the stress and the change a child brings, I am here to spill the beans on something that you may not have heard before. One of the biggest secrets in the motherhood club is: parents do not always cope. It's a fact that parents have miniature meltdowns on a regular basis and quite often have no idea what they are doing.

Yes, it's true! Even if you are physically, emotionally, and mentally ready to have a baby, there will be times when you feel like you cannot do it anymore. I have days when I have had a fair amount of sleep and seem to cope well with whatever is thrown at me, and I manage not only to get by, but to actually enjoy myself and have some fun. But there are also days when I am sleep deprived and frustrated, and it all seems too much. These are the days when my resolve falters, and just for a little while I am not able to cope; days when I simply need a decent cry.

On those days, not only does this super-organised wonder-mum sit on the floor in a gibbering heap feeling sorry for herself, she also screams her frustrations towards the heavens. And during these moments when her industrial-strength coping mechanisms come crashing down around her and she knows nothing but utter despair, she wonders if she has made the worst mistake of her life.

Then when she looks down at her delightful if somewhat demanding young girl through tear-filled eyes and tries to imagine summoning the strength to get through another hour, let alone another ten years, of motherhood, something extraordinary usually happens. As difficult as it seems at the time—as with so many other bad days and unpleasant situations she has experienced before in her life—once the tears have been shed and the universe cursed, she somehow manages to recover and return to the job at hand. And moments later she usually finds herself rolling on the floor, laughing and tickling her somewhat concerned and truly loving little princess.

Both the media and society in general have duped us into believing that we can all be superwomen, that all babies are angels, and that becoming a parent is an entirely joyous time filled only with love and laughter. Of course this is not a realistic view of motherhood, and all women need to know that whilst they may enjoy and be good at motherhood, there will be days when they won't cope, and days when they won't enjoy parenting—or even their child, if only for a few minutes. This is a normal and natural part of motherhood.

There is no way to know how well you are going to cope with having a baby until you become a parent. However, being mentally prepared for the challenging times ahead and having a realistic idea of what looking after a child will be like will certainly help. The important thing is to not let the idea of having bad days affect your decision about becoming a mum since the bad days are always outweighed by the good.

Am I doing this for the right reasons?

Many of us may enjoy being around children and like the idea of family life but aren't necessarily born with an innate longing for motherhood. Without this motherly instinct, it is really hard to know whether having a child is the right thing to do, and whether we are considering it for the right reasons. Like me, you may have had those clucky moments and thought the idea of having a couple of Mini-Mes running around might be nice—fantasies that usually faded away as you went on with your busy child-free life.

Despite the pressure you may sometimes feel from both outside influences and personal indecision, the only right reason to have a child is because you want a family of your own. To find true personal happiness we really need to understand what we want out of life and what makes us happy. We should never consider having children simply because we think we are running out of time or are worried we might live to regret it.

I spent most of my adult life being ambivalent about joining the parenting club. However, on a couple of occasions my deeply buried motherly instinct unexpectedly raised her head, and both times I was facing the real possibility of an unexpected pregnancy. It was during those very distressing and confusing times that I had to throw away all my logic and consider motherhood from a whole new and very real perspective.

If you have ever had a late or missed period, I am sure you can relate to the rollercoaster of emotions this situation can bring. Whilst these types of experiences can be frightening, they can also be useful. Think back to how you felt at the time and try to remember how you and your partner reacted to the possibility of an unplanned child. Can you recall if you were filled with joy or dread at this unexpected news? And when the pregnancy didn't eventuate, can you remember if you felt sad or relieved?

On the occasions that this happened to me, after the initial reactions of panic and fear, I started to accept the situation and think I might not make a bad mother after all. Then my period arrived and the situation resolved itself. What is interesting is that my subsequent reaction was not what I would have expected. Instead of feeling relief and joy, I felt disappointment and sadness. Without realising it, I had unexpectedly already fallen in love with this little person and the idea of becoming a mother. Instead of being happy, I felt empty and wondered for just a moment if, deep down, I wanted a family after all.

Whilst these kinds of feelings alone probably aren't strong enough reasons to stop your contraception today, they do give you some insight as to what lies in your heart and may help you come to a deeper understanding of how you feel about motherhood.

Am I selfish?

If you are considering not having a baby just because it may affect your quality of life, you may wonder if you are being selfish. And society is more than happy to tell you that you are, indeed, selfish and that it is wrong for you to want to enjoy your life and put yourself first. In fact, many people actually do think that everybody should be prepared to make the necessary sacrifices to create a new life.

Before motherhood and even now I find it difficult to accept the audacity of people who suggest that there is something wrong with you if you want to remain childless, as if there is something fundamentally unnatural about choosing individual freedom over parenthood. Family is important to most of us, but we should still have the right to decide what we want out of life, both now and in the future.

One of the big reasons that I continued to delay motherhood was that I wanted autonomy in my life. I wanted to stay up late, drink too much wine, sleep in on weekends and take off on romantic weekends at the drop of a hat. I wanted to have all my disposable income available for fancy dinners, good wine, and boots to die for. Yes! I wanted it all, and even now I can tell you quite confidently that I did not feel one bit embarrassed or guilty about my feelings—and I didn't feel selfish. To be or not to be a parent is a choice either way, and neither is selfish or unselfish. It is simply the best choice for that person at that moment.

Despite being told that we now have more choices in our lives than ever before, there is still the stigma of selfishness for women who don't provide their spouse—or mother-in-law—with the fruit of their loins. Even with all our steps forward, people still want to presume to dictate what is right for someone else, and feel entirely comfortable to openly discuss these thoughts in public. More than once, I have stood back and seen women visibly cringe after hearing comments like, "John is such a terrific guy and would make a fantastic dad. Stop being selfish, Jackie, and give the poor bloke a son."

Whether intentional or not, these types of comments are hurtful, and can chip away at your resolve. You must learn to reject suggestions that you are selfish as these are nothing more than sweeping and insensitive statements. Having a baby is never a simple and easy choice, and despite other people's well-meaning and insightful observations about John's perceived parenting skills, you will be the one carrying and raising "John's son" so it is you, and only you, who needs to be prepared to have a child. The rest of them will just have to learn to wait.

Even when you are strong in your convictions, these types of attitudes can eventually take their toll and leave you succumbing to feelings of guilt and confusion or, even worse, wondering if you are less of a woman because you don't feel maternal. When women around you start having families and you still don't feel clucky, it is easy to jump to the conclusion that you are too "selfish" or simply not feminine enough to be a mother. These feelings are perfectly normal—and perfect nonsense! Having a child is not what makes you a woman, and being a woman is not a good enough reason in itself to become a mother.

You may change your mind later on down the track, but until you are 100% convinced that the time is right for you, you need to be strong and make the decision that is right for you right now. The last thing you need is to be pressured into having a child you are not prepared for or may not even want, and end up becoming resentful towards your partner, your family, or worse still, the innocent baby in the middle of it all. It is better to be deemed "selfish" now than to ending up unhappy, divorced, and feeling trapped in a family situation that you neither wanted nor enjoy.

Fears

Probably four of the biggest commitments you will make in your life will be choosing a career, getting married, buying a house, and having a baby. Although marriage starts out as a lifetime commitment, there is always an escape hatch if things go wrong. The house can be sold, and it is now pretty common for people to change careers multiple times in the course of their working lives. That leaves having a baby, as being the only lifetime commitment that fills us with fear because it does not come with a "get out of jail free" card if we change our minds.

Of course, women are no strangers to fear. We catch trains at night, we fight for our rights at work even against intimidating managers, we travel abroad alone, and we even face up to things like finding lumps in our breasts. It is scary to face the unknown, and wonder if we are up to the task, however, women are often stronger than they think, and prove themselves in this world every day. But when it comes to having a baby, there are so many things to fear that it is worth taking time to look at some of the things you may be worried about.

What if I don't enjoy motherhood?

Do you sometimes feel like you aren't a "child person" and probably wouldn't enjoy motherhood? If so, don't let these feelings scare you off! Even though, you may not always enjoy being around other people's children or know how to handle them, it is an entirely different story when you are a parent yourself. You may be surprised to know that when it comes to your own child, your instincts kick in and you just seem to know how to handle situations the right way.

Before becoming a mother, I would walk into a restaurant and think*, oh great! There are kids here*. But the funny thing is that once I became a mother, I was amazed at how fast my thoughts and feelings changed. Most, if not all, of the things that used to worry, bore, or annoy me about children just didn't bother me anymore.

But you don't even have to enjoy other people's children to love having your own. Even now as a mother, I still find other people's children and their behaviour annoying.

Parenting will take all you have to give, and then some more. But at the same time your heart will overflow with a profound love and joy that only parents fully understand and feel. If you asked most parents—even the most tired and haggard looking among them—they will say that being a parent is a job they would not trade for anything in the world.

I'm scared!

For many of us, the decision as to whether to have a child isn't what really delays our entrance into motherhood; what really holds us back is that giving birth scares the hell out of us! And let's face it; there are a lot of things to be afraid of.

I don't know how many times I wondered whether I would be able to cope with nine months of pregnancy and all that goes with it, or whether I could manage the pain associated with childbirth. On more than one occasion I had been (mis)informed that labour is the most painful experience a human being can endure and live through, so having a baby was the most frightening thing I could imagine doing. I absolutely do not do pain well. In fact, I am one of those people who faint every time she gets a blood test.

Although I am probably at the top end of the squeamish pile, I am not the only one who has seen some all-too-graphic birth videos or been subjected to childbirth horror stories from family and friends.

It isn't just the physical act of having a baby that scares us; it is the mental and emotional aspects too. We worry about whether we will be able to cope or understand what to do once the baby arrives, and whether our partner will still find us attractive after our body has changed. Having a baby is a hard enough choice to make on its own, but with all these extra emotional and physical fears attached to it, the decision becomes that much bigger and more frightening.

Considering that I am a self-confessed baby, you may be wondering how I managed to pluck up enough courage to have one myself. Well, I didn't pluck up the courage at all. What I did instead was to resolve not to think about any of it, deciding I would simply become pregnant and then just deal with it. This meant no procrastinating and no worrying about what it would be like or how I would survive. I would learn to be brave. And that's what I did.

So, did the reality of pregnancy and childbirth match up to my fears? Yes and no. I have to admit that there was quite a lot of pain and discomfort involved, and I did faint quite a few times during my journey. And on more than one occasion I had to close my eyes and think happy thoughts.

When I got to the big event, though, I did just fine. Childbirth was definitely painful, but it was not as horrible as I had imagined, and was certainly nowhere near the "beyond the realms of human suffering" that I had once envisaged—especially after five hours of active labour when I was introduced to my new best friend, the epidural.

Whilst pregnancy and delivery were not entirely pleasant experiences for me, once I had someone so tiny and precious to care for, and such an incredible reason to be brave, I surprised myself and found all the courage I needed. I made it through labour and childbirth without swearing; I didn't shed a single tear; and I didn't even come close to fainting. Once upon a time, I never would have believed that I could have done it, but now I can proudly say that I have. So, for all you scaredy cats out there, know that if I can do it, there is hope for you yet.

Will I be a good mum?

We are surrounded by so many images and idealisations of "good mothers", it's no wonder many women doubt they have what it takes to be a decent parent. When I was growing up, I was a second mother to my three younger sisters. Even back then I knew in my heart that, if I chose to be, I could be a darned good mother one day. But that experience alone was not enough to stop me from constantly worrying about one day becoming a mother. By the time I was contemplating a family of my own, it had been twenty years since I had spent any real time around babies.

But on the day that I first held my daughter, I was so overwhelmed with love that I realised that I would and could do whatever it took to give her a happy and healthy home. When it came time to leave the hospital, I pushed off the uncertainty and fear and did what I do best—I read and studied everything I could get my hands on. Taking the time to research, read, and talk to other mums bolstered my confidence, and it wasn't long before every tidbit of information I had ever heard about young children came flooding back to me as my maternal instincts switched into overdrive.

Despite all those facts and knowledge, what I really learned was that motherhood is a hands-on job to be learnt on my feet, and quickly. It was hard in the beginning, but I was surprised at how fast I went from being someone who looked at veteran mums with envy to someone others came to for advice.

So, how can you possibly know whether you will be a good mum? All parents are human, and no matter what our background, we will all face the same trials and tribulations and experience the same doubts, fears, and disappointments. You already know that being a parent will be hard, and that it can be the most rewarding and wondrous thing you will ever do in your life. If you have a realistic idea of the time and effort that goes into raising a child, and couple this knowledge with patience and a big heart, the love you will have for your child alone will be all you need to get started. Everything else will come in time, and you will probably be surprised at how natural parenting is when it is your own child. To let you in on a little secret, most of us parents are just winging it no matter how confident and in control we might appear. Parenting has and always will be a day-to-day learning process that is full of both challenges and surprises. And lucky for all of us, children are extremely forgiving. Remember that there will always be a tomorrow in which to do better.

Will I become my mother?

As hard as it is to accept, I am starting to sound like my mother. I already call people only a few years younger than me "kids" and am always reminiscing about how much better and cheaper things were in "my day". As much as I try to avoid the subject, the reality is I am growing up. And as awful as it sounds, instead of yelling "Have fun!" as my daughter races off on her latest adventure, I find myself calling, "Put your jacket on before you get cold." When you still feel young and rebellious at heart, it is sometimes difficult to imagine turning into a mum who spoils the fun by pointing out all the evident and potential dangers, or one who is always close by with a tissue and some heart-felt advice. But like it or not, most women find themselves saying and doing the things they swore they would never do or say to their own child.

Becoming a mother is a learnt venture, and for some of us, growing up to be just like our mothers would be an achievement to be proud of. For others, it might be a nightmare. Whilst it is easy to assume that the mere act of having a child will turn you into your mother, the reality is that no matter how you were raised or how much your mother's influence has defined the woman you are today, you will still always be *you*. Sure, some of your mum's parenting style may rub off on you, but you will find that you essentially become a more capable version of the person you are now.

On the other hand, you may find valid reasons behind many of your mother's choices and much of her advice. Once you begin to walk in her shoes for a while, you may start to look at her a whole lot differently—and you may finally begin to understand both her and her choices a little better.

What will people think if I don't have kids?

If you have ever told people that you have decided not to have children, then you are probably familiar with the patronising response of, "You'll change your mind", especially if you are of a certain age and in a stable relationship. You've probably also heard the ominous warning, "You'll regret it." Other reactions can range from surprise and jealousy to downright anger.

I don't think people mean to be so rude; it's that childbearing is so ingrained into our understanding of what women do that people often find it difficult to understand why someone would choose not to have kids. Try as you might, you will never be able to change the opinions of others, and you certainly cannot change the long-standing social expectations that all women have a responsibility to have children. But despite the anxiety others feel at your decision, you must always remember that the choice is yours.

What if I change my mind later on?

During my research phase, I came across a study that discussed recent research into the happiness of older women who had chosen to stay child-free. After interviewing thousands of women, the study concluded that a massive seventy-five per cent of them had regretted their decision not to have a family. The results genuinely shocked me, and I immediately took the information to heart. The figures made me think long and hard about whether I wanted to let the opportunity to have children pass me by. Being a numbers girl, I ended up being persuaded by the data that essentially told me that ninety-six per cent of women wanted to be mothers and that there was a seventy-five per cent chance that I would regret my choice if I decided not to have a baby. Of course, the main reasons for my decision were a lot wiser and more heartfelt than cold numerical facts, but this information did eventually help me answer a simple question: *Is there a strong chance that I will regret my decision not to have a baby if I change my mind later?* From the research I had done, I knew the answer would more than likely be yes!

Most of us understand that our chances of conceiving decrease with each passing year, and that once we reach a certain age, our fertility begins to drop dramatically. If you have been or still are hesitant and do decide to leave baby-making until the second part of your childbearing years, you would not be alone; however, there are still a few things to think about if you decide to wait.

Despite the stories of women giving birth at age sixty and improvements in in-vitro fertilisation (IVF), women should not rely on this as a way to have it all now and delay motherhood until they are absolutely sure. Assisted fertility is expensive, can make you sick, and traditionally has a remarkably small percentage of positive outcomes. If you are concerned about changing your mind later on or leaving it too late and would like to conceive naturally, then you should consider getting started sooner rather than later. If for some reason you still miss that all-important baby boat and end up feeling a gap in your life, you may be able to look at such options as egg donation, adoption, or fostering.

Remember that motherhood isn't the only way to feel fulfilled. Working with the homeless or with sick children, or dedicating time to other worthwhile interests and hobbies that fill your life with joy and meaning can go a long way towards a happy life. Whatever you choose, think long and hard about what you want out of life and don't delay your decision too long. We all know that this is the one choice we need to get right and that it's all in the timing!

What if I still have doubts after I am pregnant?

I admit that whilst I was one hundred per cent sure of my decision to have a baby, and was over the moon when I saw those two little pink lines, there were many days during my pregnancy that I had doubts. Some days it was just the same old questions and fears that I had experienced before becoming pregnant, but on other days, on the extremely difficult days, I would think to myself, *what on earth have I done?*

Pregnancy and motherhood is often painted as being nothing short of pure bliss, but, unfortunately, this is not always the case. Despite the perfectly normal ups and downs that any pregnancy entails, it seems that the media and even many women still prefer to promote the fantasy rather than discuss the dark side of being pregnant. This oversight only serves to give women an unrealistic view of what to expect, which leads to discouraged mothers-to-be full of feelings of inadequacy.

These types of feelings can cause women to doubt their decision. However, having been there, I can assure you that these doubts are normal, and having them does not mean you are unfit for motherhood. Having fears and doubts and steadily growing to love your baby over time are the most natural things in the world. I certainly wasn't always the happy, vibrant woman we see in the movies and often hated being pregnant but this didn't stop me from enjoying the result.

From the time I looked down to see those two life-changing pink lines to the thrilling moment when I saw my baby on the big screen for the first time, I experienced some real issues with my maternal instinct and had some grave concerns about whether I had made the right decision. But once I found out my babies sex, and was able to choose her name and talk to her as a real person, I felt a maternal bond and a love that will be with us both for life and beyond.

This is such a powerful and generally undiscussed matter and is one of the founding reasons for my decision to share my personal pregnancy journal. What you will find throughout my journey is that, with any big change, there will always be fears and doubts. But like any new experience, you need to work through it and take both the good with the bad. And in the case of pregnancy, I was rewarded with the most wondrous gift of all: my own Mini-Me.

There are no guarantees in life, and every decision we make comes with a certain amount of calculated risk. If you are still unsure about whether you will enjoy parenting, all I can suggest is that you do your research. Read parenting magazines to see what kind of issues parents have to deal with these days, and spend some time with families with both young and older children to make sure you have a clear understanding of what family life is all about.

Then if you think parenting is something you could learn to love, stop procrastinating, take the plunge, and do what millions of other couples do worldwide every year: board the baby boat!

Chapter 6

The Good, the Bad, and the Fun Reasons to Have a Baby

Why do I want to have a baby? is probably the most fundamental question you need to ask yourself. Carefully examining your reasons for wanting a child and ensuring those reasons are both valid and positive will definitely help you make the right choice. The reasons people choose to have children will vary, but you will find that most women have probably had some of the same thoughts as you. Let's take a look at some of the good, bad, and fun reasons to dive into parenthood.

Some not so good reasons

Often we look at a young child and see a sweet, innocent, precious little being and forget that the adorable baby also means significant and long-lasting lifestyle changes. Parenthood is not a decision to be taken lightly, so let's discuss some of the reasons why right now may *not* be the best time to start a family.

To fix a troubled relationship

If your relationship is rocky, having a baby may seem like a great idea to bring you and your partner closer. Unfortunately, this scheme seldom works; in fact, it often has the opposite effect and now not only do you have a bad relationship, but there's an innocent child caught up in the mix.

Having a baby is stressful and puts extra pressure on even the strongest and happiest of couples. If you are serious about starting a family, then you will need to sort out any differences in the relationship beforehand, especially if you have a high-stress situation like being worried your partner might leave you.

Remember that being pregnant and having a baby is not going to change who your partner is or who *you* are, nor how willing either of you are to fix or commit to the relationship. A child deserves a happy and safe home where she or he is wanted and loved by both parents. Ironing out the creases in your relationship before you decide to have a baby means you will go into parenthood as a united team and be rewarded with greater success and happiness.

To get a partner to settle down

Sometimes when a woman is sick of waiting for her partner to "catch up" to her in the relationship, she may wonder what would happen if she accidentally "forgot" to take her birth control pills. Could a surprise baby be all she needs to get her wayward boyfriend to change his ways and become the devoted, loving father and husband she has always dreamed of?

Whilst anything is possible, this is a high-risk manoeuvre. Imagine the potential outcomes:

> Your partner is thrilled and asks you to marry him. But don't get excited, this is a long shot and the odds are stacked against you!
>
> Your partner finds out you manipulated him and the situation to pressure him to commit. He feels betrayed and resentful not only of you, but of his unborn child. This leads to the end of the relationship and the beginning of your life as a single parent.
>
> Your wayward partner decides that having a baby might be a lark but has no intention of changing his ways or being a hands-on father and supporting his family. You end up

a pseudo single parent to a baby and an oversized child in an environment non-conducive to either raising a child or nurturing a committed relationship.

No matter how much your heart may ache for a husband and child, if your partner is not willing to settle down or is telling you that he isn't ready, then you need to listen to him. Starting a family requires that you both be committed and ready for the changes to your lifestyle. Forcing him into the situation will not make him a more willing and capable father, make him grow up any faster or improve your relationship. Only time and age will bring him closer to being ready—or to leaving. But if he is the one for you and you want a future together, you will just have to tread water and wait until the time is right for you both.

To enjoy unconditional love

It is only human nature to want to feel loved and needed, and it is easy to assume that a child can bring us the love and purpose that we may be missing in our lives. Whilst it is true that your child will love you unconditionally, filling a perceived void is not a solid reason for entering into motherhood.

Life has its ups and downs: moments of loneliness and depression, and moments of joy, both of which we would like to share with someone. But having a baby cannot be about filling emotional gaps in your life. Not only is it a selfish reason, but it also puts too much pressure on the child. Having a baby is so much more than the lifetime bond between mother and child; it is about giving yourself over completely and selflessly to another human being.

And strangely enough, despite the twenty-four hour responsibility of motherhood, having a baby can sometimes make you feel even lonelier since you are often stuck at home on your own with a demanding child, no support, and no adult conversation. Instead of feeling loved, you could be left feeling even more miserable than before.

If you are feeling lost or lonely and think there is something missing from your life, then it is important for you to find your own happiness first. That way when the time is right, you will be able to unconditionally return all the love and attention your new little bundle of joy will bestow upon you.

I'm running out of time

In the words of Benjamin Franklin, "You may delay, but time will not."

Many of us start out thinking that marriage and kids will just happen and that we have all the time in the world to get everything we want done. But time is a funny thing; it often moves faster than we expect. It seems that one minute we are leaving school and setting off into the world, and the next we are saying, "Oh sh*t, I forgot to have kids!" Suddenly all that time we thought we had is gone and our gynaecologist is reminding us that we are not getting any younger.

Like it or not, the pressure to make the baby decision before it is too late is all too common and is the reason this book was conceived in the first place. As an older mother, I know firsthand the pressure and panic that you probably encounter every time another birthday rolls around, and how suddenly you only have a small amount of time to make an extremely large decision.

I am sure you already understand the importance of bringing a child into a financially and emotionally secure environment; however, it is even more crucial that this same child is born into this world because he or she is truly wanted. If this is the first time you are asking yourself the baby question, then you need to do this independently of Mother Nature's eternal stopwatch. Honestly answer the question: "If I haven't wanted a child for the past twenty years, why do I suddenly want one now?"

Don't get me wrong, I do understand that a loudly ticking biological clock can be a persuasive motivator. However, when you decide to have a baby, it needs to be because you want one and not just because time is running out. Don't let the fear of getting too old to have a baby cloud your decision. Remember that despite your concerns about future regrets, your ticking biological clock can quickly turn into a loud alarm clock that goes off every two hours for a feed and nappy change.

Everyone else is

I am sure most of us wouldn't mind "keeping up with the Kardashians", and we have all felt the odd pang of jealousy or longing for what others may have. Some of us may even be guilty of buying something just to fit in, look cool, or to do what everyone else is doing. Whilst buying the latest smart phone or widescreen TV, may make you feel more in vogue, having a child "for show" is never a smart idea.

The glamorous and fun image of parenthood that we are bombarded with from ads and magazines belies the full reality that kids need all your attention, are expensive, and take up most of your physical and emotional energy. If your circle of friends is suddenly arranging play dates and discussing the best preschools, you may feel left out, but that is certainly no reason to join the fray. If you aren't truly ready or willing to take on all aspects of parenthood, then you are probably not ready to follow the pack just yet.

There is nothing wrong with waiting—and even if you do end up being the only couple in your social circle that doesn't have children, does it really matter? Don't allow yourself to be pressured into having children just to "fit in". If you want to be a happy mum with a happy child, you must wait until the time is right for you. In the meantime, you can practice on your best friend's baby and enjoy being their favourite aunt or uncle for a while longer.

To repair an unhappy childhood

Sometimes people from dysfunctional families or those who have had an unhappy childhood swear off ever having children simply because they have no happy memories of family life. Others, however, become determined to one day be the perfect parent and correct their own upbringing by "doing things right".

Whilst having an unhappy childhood may make you a more understanding and loving mother, choosing to compensate for a miserable youth by having a child should not be your sole reason for wanting a family.

In these situations, be careful that you do not have unrealistic ideas about how having a baby may resolve your past pain. No matter how fantastic your child makes your life, she or he will not eliminate a negative or unhappy childhood. There is certainly nothing wrong with striving to be a fabulous mum as long as the time is right and you are ready. Once you reach that point, then yes, your past experiences should give you a clear understanding of the type of parent you want to be—and you will probably have a head start when it comes to the kind of mistakes you would like to avoid.

To recapture my youth

If you grew up wanting to be a world-famous actress or sportsman but were never able to realise this goal, you may think that with the right encouragement and guidance, your own child might one day accomplish some of your lifelong dreams. As enjoyable as it is to have some common interests in the family, we must learn to accept that sometimes dreams do pass us by, and we should never force our own desires and passions onto someone else or try to live our lives through them.

You have your own dreams and goals, and your child as an individual will have his or her own dreams and goals that may not match yours. Your kids may even grow up to be nothing like you, or even feel the need to rebel against your wishes in an effort to become more independent. Every person is an individual with his or her own appearance, temperament, strengths, and weaknesses, and your child has the right to grow into the person she or he was meant to be. Having a child in order to fulfil *your* dreams can only lead to disappointment for you and crushing pressure for your child.

I don't want to end up alone

In our youth, we are usually surrounded by friends and family, and imagine that it will always be so. But life has a way of surprising us, sometimes unpleasantly, and it is frightening to think what it would be like to be left alone in our later years.

Being surrounded by family is an excellent way to imagine your future retirement, but you would be taking an enormous risk if your only reason for having children is so that you do not end up alone. Having children does not guarantee that they will be around in your twilight years. Whilst some close-knit families have the luxury of living in the same city, the harsh reality is that with global employment and bustling modern lives, many families may only get together once or twice a year, and in some circumstances not at all simply because they don't get along. As enjoyable as it is to be surrounded by family, your retirement plan certainly shouldn't include making your children or grandchildren your only source of companionship and entertainment. You would do better to cultivate other interests and relationships; and in that case, having family that visits often would be icing on the cake.

Good Reasons

A huge part of our personal histories involve family, and in a big world, family can be a touchstone—a safe place, a happy place, and a place where you belong. Creating your own family is undeniably an incredible and natural part of being human.

There is nothing like the togetherness that family brings. If somewhere deep down you have always thought you were meant to be a mother and were destined to guide a little person through life, then listen to your heart, stop worrying about sleepless nights and nappy changes, and start thinking about trips to the zoo and all those fun-filled play dates.

So let's leave the negative reasons behind and look at some of the good reasons for having children.

To create my own family

Becoming a parent is an innate desire for most people, and our nurturing instinct and dreams of creating our own family usually start early in life. Most women will remember playing mummies and daddies when they were little girls, and spending countless hours mothering their favourite toy, all in preparation for creating a family of their own.

Imagine how beautiful it would be to have those fond memories become a reality by having a little person to love who not only talks back, but who might even look a bit like you. The possibility of creating a new life, someone with his or her own unique personality, a little person who you can love and live with whilst she or he grows and develops into an adult is as strong a pull as any I have ever known.

If you have fond memories of your own childhood, have always loved being around children, and have dreamed of raising and nurturing your own little ankle-biter, then it may be time to start thinking about what you and your partner may have to give a child, and whether you are at the right time and place in order to make this dream a reality.

It could be fun

As a parent, you will have a little dependent person who needs your attention 24/7. You will also need to spend time teaching him or her about the world and steering him or her in the right direction. But no one says you can't have a little fun along the way—and yes, parenting *can* be fun! It's the perfect opportunity by which to recapture your youth and once again experience all the classic experiences of childhood.

Children's happiness is contagious. After living through years of the drudgery of mainstream adult life, I am now thoroughly enjoying life with a young child. Most days I find myself getting excited and looking forward to the simplest of activities, just because I know how much fun my daughter will derive from it.

Think about the joy you will experience as you watch your kids fall in love with Bert and Ernie, eat their first ice cream, and eventually begin staying up late to catch a glimpse of Santa and his reindeer. And the fun won't stop there; there will be the first bike, the first ocean swim, and the first time on a swing. And then there is the joy of watching their first steps, or the day your heart melts when they say "Mummy" for the first time or fold their arms around you and say, "I love you."

As their tour guide in life, you get to open their eyes to a whole new world. You will have loads of fun showing them things for the first time and helping them discover some of the greater pleasures in life like music, dancing, art, and food. Now who would want to miss out on a fun-filled itinerary like that?

Your social life could get a boost

If your life has become predictable and seems to be missing something, then becoming a parent could be nothing but positive for you as it opens up a whole new world and a whole new set of friends. When you become a mother, you automatically become a member of the world's biggest club. Once you start pushing a stroller, you suddenly become the focus of other mums and dads, and you will be relatively quickly and usually quite warmly welcomed with open arms.

Since becoming a mum, I have met a lovely group of friends at ante-natal classes, at the midwife clinics, in the nursery section of shopping centres, and in the queue at the supermarket. What is great about meeting these new people is that they are all following the same path as me and have become my sanity and my sounding board through the passage of raising children.

The other neat thing about motherhood is that you get out and about a lot more and start re-experiencing all those incredible parts of being a child that you may have forgotten. Once your Saturday mornings stop being about sleeping in to nurse a giant hangover or cleaning the house to a military standard, you will be able to start enjoying sunshine-filled day trips and lattes in the park.

In between swimming lessons, ballet classes, and cheering your kids on at the footy ground, you will rarely have time to get bored and will probably get a whole new lease on life.

It is a good time financially

It has been a long time coming, but finally having babies has been recognised as an important role in Australian society. Our government has even encouraged us to have kids to bolster the dwindling birth rates. You are probably familiar with former Treasurer Peter Costello's now famous phrase: "All women should have three children—one for Mum, one for Dad, and one for the country."

Thanks to this recognition, most of us will now get some kind of financial assistance, be it paid maternity leave, the baby bonus, or the family tax benefit. With additional financial aid, many women can now feel more confident in their ability to take time off work to have babies and raise their children, without worrying about how they are going to put food on the table. And it doesn't stop there, further support for working parents includes special care leave days and childcare tax rebates.

Flexible work arrangements have also become easier to access thanks to new legislation introduced under the Fair Work Act 2009, which allows all employees to request flexible working arrangements as part of the Australian National Employment Standards. The legislation has been specifically designed to assist individuals and employers in finding more work-life balance and will be an enormous advantage to working mothers.

If you think you are ready to start a family, sit down and do the sums. If you can financially afford to have a baby, take advantage of these benefits whilst they are still available. Even a little bit of extra help can make that time off work seem a lot less scary!

Being a stay-at-home parent is now okay

Fortunately for women today, we have lived through the days of staunch feminism where women not only felt it was their right but actually wanted to and looked forward to becoming a career mum, and being a stay-at-home mum was considered backward and frowned upon by elements of the feminist movement. We can also be thankful for the long-ago demise of the fifties housewife who was expected to stay home to cook and clean.

Like all things, times and attitudes change, and the way in which the family unit works and supports itself has changed too. Women, and now some men, no longer have to feel embarrassed or ashamed about staying home to raise their children.

In fact, being a stay-at-home parent has become the latest trend and the preferred situation for many people. I can certainly vouch for this change in attitude, since all my new mummy friends, who once had thriving careers and every intention of going back to work halfway through their baby's first year, have now fully embraced the joys of motherhood and spent the first year of their child's life dreading going back to work. Of all the career mums in my ante-natal class, only two of us have rejoined the workforce, and in both cases only on a part-time basis.

It isn't just women with this newfound attitude; men are also swapping suits and ties and board meetings for biscuit baking and play dates. I have quite a few male friends who have become a part of this phenomenon, giving up their well-paid careers to raise their children whilst their wives go back to work. Not only are these men proud of their new roles, but they continuously brag to anyone who will listen about how enjoyable being a stay-at-home dad is.

The other great thing I have discovered is that stay-at-home mums and dads no longer need to feel as isolated as they once did, thanks to a network of web communities, chat rooms, and parenting groups that offer friendship, advice, and support. Technology means that the outside world is only a click away.

Many new parents are also enjoying the benefits of combining their career with child-raising by finding jobs that allow them to work from home some or all of the time. Some are dusting off their entrepreneurial skills and starting their own home business. And that's exactly what I did. Instead of using my maternity leave to read Women's magazines and watch soap operas, I spent my time writing this book and creating a website, both in the hope of finding a way to spend more time at home with my family.

I am ready for a new challenge

You have a strong relationship with your husband or partner and make an excellent team. You have the house, the job, and the car, and the pages of your passports are looking pretty full. You have worked through and succeeded in many of life's challenges. With your finances and health stable, it is only natural to believe that it may be time to move on to the next chapter in your life. If you have made a dent in your bucket list and feel ready for the many challenges and compromises that a baby brings, and are prepared to handle everything from nappy changes to talks about "where do I come from", then, yes you may be ready for this challenge of a lifetime.

More fun reasons

People are quick to tell you the worst parts of parenting, but what most parents fail to mention is that parenting isn't all tantrums, dirty nappies, and sleepless nights. Rather, it is often filled with laughter and can really be a hoot. Here is a quick rundown of other fun reasons to have a baby.

> You have an excuse as to why you aren't "bikini ready" this summer.
> You don't have to borrow someone else's kid whenever you want to watch the latest Disney movie.
> You finally get some of those family tax benefits.
> You have an excuse for not having the housework done.

You get to see the world through a child's eyes and can stop being so cynical all the time.

You get to blame things on your baby, like being late or not being able to attend an event.

Toys, toys, and more toys. If you want the new Xbox One, you've got a superb reason to buy it.

You get to relive your childhood—think circus, theme parks, water slides, and the zoo.

You have someone who will laugh at your jokes, even the lame ones.

You will have someone who thinks your singing voice is incredible, and that you are the world's best dancer.

You get to have lots of fun doing all the things that are just for kids, like watching cartoons on Saturday mornings, eating ice cream at 10 am, and jumping in puddles with the sole aim of getting covered in mud.

And the best and most fun parts that we all already know: the Tooth Fairy, Easter egg hunts, birthday parties, Halloween, and our all-time favourite, Christmas. Who doesn't love seeing the joy in children's eyes during these special times?

Chapter 7

Physical, Financial and Practical Concerns

Physical Concerns

Once you have thought about your reasons for wanting a child and have decided that it may be the right thing for you, you then need to consider whether your body is up to the task of getting you through pregnancy and childbirth.

Having a baby is hard work physically, so before you even get started you should consider doing some research into your family's medical history to determine if there are any known medical problems, particularly issues that may relate to your fertility or your ability to carry to full term or deliver naturally.

Even if we feel young, our bodies are ageing on the inside, and as we grow older things do get harder. Our bodies just don't cope quite as well as they did in our youth. So, if you are serious about starting a family, then this is the perfect time for both you and your partner to undergo some medical tests to ensure you are both physically well, and to check that neither of you has any illnesses that could affect the baby before or after the birth. Planning a family is the perfect excuse to start getting into shape or kicking a few vices if your health isn't quite what it should be.

Can you physically have a baby?

There is more to starting a family than making the decision to have a baby. One of the big things that people often forget is that no matter how much you might desire a child, it will actually come down to whether you can physically have one.

When you are not consciously trying to conceive, you don't worry about your fertility or stop to think that it could take twelve months or more to fall pregnant. Most of us assume that when we are finally ready, it will just happen—BOOM!

It can take such a long time for many of us to get past the psychological issues surrounding motherhood, and we are so focused on the "do we want to" aspects of having a baby that we often forget about the physical aspects. Let's take a look at the everyday health issues that could affect your ability to have children, some of which you might already know about and others that might surprise you.

Your weight

Not many women realise this, but when it comes to getting pregnant your current weight makes a difference. Being over or underweight can not only have a tremendous impact on your current fertility but also affect your chances of miscarrying or carrying your child to full term.

To increase your chances of becoming pregnant and reduce the chances of miscarriage or premature birth, it will be beneficial for both you and your partner to get your weight issues under control now. Not only does taking control of your health make a significant difference before trying for a baby, it is also in your own best interest long term.

For me, knowing I could be carrying around an extra fifteen kilos was enough to make reaching a pre-pregnancy weight that I was generally happy with one of my first goals. By improving my fitness and losing a few extra kilos, I hoped that my improved lifestyle would not only increase my chances of a healthy pregnancy but would also help me get my pre-baby body back.

Fortunately for me, incorporating some additional exercise into my life, switching to light beer, and giving up those delicious pre-mix cans of bourbon and coke enabled me to lose five kilograms during my preconception care period. This not only improved my health but gave me a significant head start towards getting back into my jeans afterwards.

Your back

We have all seen images of heavily pregnant women holding their backs in discomfort but it isn't just pregnancy and labour you need to worry about. Motherhood in general takes an enormous toll on your back, and during the first year your back will be working overtime. Not only will you spend hours bent over a cot patting and rocking your baby to sleep, but you will also be constantly feeding and carrying your baby for hours at a time. With this kind of workload, even the healthiest of postures is going to feel the strain.

It is also worth considering the impact a weak back may have on your ability to deliver naturally. Often women with back problems are forced into early bed rest and in some cases encouraged to have a Caesarean. Having a baby is a very physical job, so if you do have any concerns about the condition or strength of your back, consult your doctor now.

Even if you don't have any known problems, there are a few things that all women can do to improve their chances of a healthy pregnancy and birth, like incorporating back-strengthening exercises into their gym routines and participating in proper posture enhancer activities like Pilates and yoga. Just like getting your weight under control, fixing any issues with your back now will be beneficial to you and your child, in the long run.

Diabetes

Diabetes affects a growing number of people around the world each year and is one condition that can not only affect your ability to become pregnant, but your ability to carry a baby full term and give birth naturally. Even if you are a fit and healthy woman with no history of diabetes, be aware that it is common for women to develop gestational diabetes during their pregnancy, which can put both themselves and their growing child at risk.

High blood sugar can affect the pregnancy in a number of ways, including your child putting on too much weight, labour being induced early, or being forced into delivering via a C-section. Due to a family history of gestational diabetes on my mother's side, I had firsthand experience with this issue and had to be strictly monitored throughout my pregnancy. At the time I hated watching my chocolate intake, and undergoing extra blood tests, however, it was an essential to help ensure that my baby and I were okay.

All women want a healthy pregnancy, so if you have or suspect you may have diabetes, it is vital that you discuss this issue with your doctor before you become pregnant.

High blood pressure

You may think that high blood pressure will only be an issue when your little prince or princess becomes a teenager. But your blood pressure can be a problem during your pregnancy and will be one of the tests, along with testing the sugar in your urine, which will be carried out at every doctor's visit.

Whilst pregnancy is natural, it is also strenuous, and your body and internal organs will be put under tremendous strain for the good part of nine months. I once read that the effort it takes for a pregnant woman to sit on the couch and breathe is similar to the effort required to climb a mountain. Add to that the emotional stress of being pregnant and the anxiety surrounding the birthing of a healthy baby, and you will begin to see why an expectant mother's blood pressure begins to rise.

One of the biggest reasons high blood pressure is a concern during pregnancy is that it can cause premature birth. Two friends of mine were diagnosed with preeclampsia and forced into early bed rest only twenty-eight weeks into their pregnancies. On both occasions, even extra rest and the proper medical care were not enough to stop both of them from going into labour two weeks later. And even with access to state-of-the-art neonatal services, I think that it is the goal of all women to carry their baby to full-term. It is frightening to think that high blood pressure or conditions like preeclampsia can and do occur in healthy, active, non-smoking women with no history of blood pressure problems.

For most of my life I had lived with low blood pressure and was totally shocked at thirty-four weeks gestation to be diagnosed with pregnancy-induced high blood pressure. Having seen what my friends had gone through, I was quite worried. My doctor advised me to rest, watch my stress levels, and come in for regular checks. Luckily for me, this was enough and I was able to continue to full term without medication or any other treatment; however, my blood pressure did spiral out of control during my labour, reaching dangerous levels and forcing me to re-evaluate my birth plan.

Of course, pregnancy affects us all differently, and high blood pressure won't be a problem for most women. Since high blood pressure can have unexpected ramifications, though, it's still a good idea to get yourself checked out before becoming pregnant as well as having regular checks throughout your pregnancy.

Your menstrual cycle

There are quite a few issues that affect a woman's cycle that can also affect her fertility. When a woman experiences difficulty conceiving, testing may reveal long-standing problems such as PCOS (Polycystic Ovary Syndrome) or endometriosis. Whilst both of these issues can usually be helped with medical assistance, it can be frustrating and disappointing to discover this news twelve months down the track after trying and failing to conceive. It can feel like you have wasted a whole year of your life.

Receiving news like this would be disconcerting for most couples, but for those eager to start a family as soon as possible, it can be disheartening and a real drawback, especially for older women who do not have time on their side. If you have a history of extremely painful or irregular periods and think that you may have issues with your cycle, consult your doctor sooner rather than later to save time and prevent future heartache.

Unknown fertility issues

Regardless of your current health, having your fertility and your partner's fertility tested early on could save you a lot of time, energy, and frustration. As disappointing as it can be to find out that you may require medical intervention or, even worse, that one of you is infertile, the news can be even more devastating if discovered after a year or two of failed baby-making attempts. And as hard as it will be to accept at the time, it is probably better knowing the truth earlier whilst there is still time to consider other options, rather than finding out when it may be too late to do anything about it.

Energy levels

If your goal is to be an active, hands-on parent, then you will need lots of energy to play and run around for hours at a time, as well as a reserve of energy to help you function on very little sleep. It also pays to remember that parenting will not be your only job; most of us will still need to hold down a job, run a household, and put time and effort into our other relationships.

To help you decide if you will have the energy to parent a small child, think about how your life is now. Do you collapse on the couch every night and all weekend, exhausted after a busy week at work? Or are you able to pursue other activities at the end of the day because you still have the energy to burn? Only you know your personal physical strength and endurance, how much energy you have in stock, and how well you do after a couple of nights of little to no sleep.

If you are lethargic by nature or are already exhausted from coping with your current life, a new baby is only going to make the situation that much more difficult, and your ability to cope is going to fall dramatically. Of course, this doesn't mean that you *won't* be able to cope, just that, like me, you may find parenting doable but exhausting. Even if you are a bit of a couch potato, don't be too concerned as even self-confessed "energizer bunnies" have days when they totally run out of puff and wonder how they will make it through the day.

For me, parenting is a lot like being on a deadline or in a crisis situation; I have to jump in and do what needs to get done. For the most part, I run on pure adrenaline, and the rest of the time on love and fresh air. And just as I always find room for dessert moments after proclaiming I couldn't eat another thing, I always find just a little bit more patience and energy when my daughter looks up at me with her beautiful, big, brown eyes and smiles.

Your pain threshold

I don't think anyone can think about having a baby without wondering how much childbirth may hurt—and I'm sure I am not the only woman in the world who has delayed motherhood for this reason alone. Unfortunately, no matter how daunting the idea of giving birth is, there is no way of getting around it. If you want to have a baby, you are going to have to suffer some pain.

Luckily, there is a lot more choice for pain relief then there used to be, so you will have options. Unlike our grandmothers who had to grin and bear it, expectant mothers can now make delivery easier and less painful with a vast range of options, from water births and hypnosis to natural pain-reducing machines like TENS, as well as gas, pethidine, and the mother of all pain relief, an epidural.

As labour is both a physical and psychological fear, and one of the biggest concerns faced by women, I have dedicated a section of this book to discussing what childbirth was like for me. Whilst every birth is different and everyone's pain threshold is different, I hope that receiving some insight from the biggest sooky baby on earth—me—will help you understand what childbirth is like and help you realise that whilst the prospect is definitely daunting, it is certainly doable.

Relationship Concerns

Human beings are sociable by nature, and we have many types of relationships in our lives: with our partner, with family and friends, and with work colleagues and acquaintances. Although the dynamics of a relationship naturally change over time, nothing alters your relationship with people as much as having a baby. A child truly does change you and how you interact with the world and those around you.

Whilst your friends and work colleagues will get used to seeing you in a different light, it is often the personal relationship with your partner that is most affected. Having a baby and becoming parents will directly impact your day-to-day lives, which, while fantastic, can also be extremely stressful and put a tremendous strain on both of you. That's why it is vital to consider the strength of your relationship before adding children into the mix.

However, if you are in a long-term, committed, and harmonious relationship in which you have good communication, lots of love for each other, and similar expectations about what you want from your future together, then you should have the right foundation on which to build a family.

How do relationships change?

Adding a third person to the intimate world of a couple is undeniably going to change the dynamics of the relationship and how each person sees the other. What is also fascinating and often overlooked is the new way in which an expectant mother is seen by her family and friends. Many women find that once they are pregnant or have had their child, their old friends start to treat them differently, and in some cases may even begin to exclude them from the more "non-family" events.

Even at work, new parents may find themselves treated differently since people may believe that their priorities and focus have changed now that they have the distractions and responsibilities of parenthood to cope with. For that same reason, new mothers are often excluded from consideration for promotions and more challenging tasks requiring overtime simply because colleagues think they have changed.

Once you start a family, you may also see the relationship with your parents change as you begin to understand what parenting is all about. That can definitely make you see your parents in a new light and deepen your understanding of them and the choices they made with you when you were growing up. Likewise, your parents, siblings, and even in-laws will now see you in a new role, which may also result in a shift in the family dynamics. In some cases, family members who played a relatively small role in your lives may want to be more involved now that there's a grandchild, niece, or nephew in the mix.

Talking about having kids

It is easy to talk generally about having kids, but a day will eventually come when you will need to sit down with your partner and speak honestly about whether you want to start a family. Once the issue is raised, the result won't always be as simple as deciding whether to have children; you will also need to consider timing, how many you want, and what kind of parents you want to be. You may find that even though you and your partner seem to agree on most things in life, when it comes to child raising, you might both have very different views. You may even have differing opinions on what you would do if you discovered something was wrong with the pregnancy, a very delicate and highly relevant issue that should be addressed when the time is right.

Discussions about having children can bring to light the differences between a couple, so try to find a time when you are both not distracted or stressed out by other issues so you can devote your full attention to talking about your hopes and expectations. That way, when the time is right, you will both be on the same page and can enter into parenthood with a united front.

What if only one of us wants kids?

If you find yourself in a situation in which you are ready to start a family but your partner is not, then you need to express to him how you are feeling and, in doing so, be willing to accept his feelings too. If, after all your discussions, the subject is still left up in the air, then you will need to determine whether your partner isn't ready now or if he will never be ready. For married couples, this would ideally have been a topic you discussed beforehand so you should know where his heart is on the subject. However, if it is something that you have only ever briefly touched upon, then you need to sit down and talk about what you both hope to get out of life.

These conversations are never easy or short. If, when you start exploring the subject, you realise that your partner has a long list of valid reasons why he shouldn't have children yet, and you are at a loss to find compelling reasons why he *should* have kids now, then the discussion could go back and forth indefinitely with no satisfactory outcome for either of you.

The decision to have a child is complicated, but is one that must come directly from the heart. It is usually quite difficult to change people's true feelings, and next to impossible if they have their heart set against something. This situation could easily degenerate into constant battles and put a tremendous strain on your usually happy relationship.

If it feels like you are always arguing about the subject, going around in circles and not making any ground, then it may be time to take a "time out" from the topic and focus on the positive parts of your relationship. Try spending some time improving your levels of communication and intimacy and maybe working on some of your other life goals. If, after attempting to broach the subject again, you fall right back into the same arguments then you may want to talk to an external party. There are many people you can turn to in these situations, from relationship counsellors to a representative from your local church. Sometimes an independent and unbiased opinion can help you both see the problem objectively.

If parenthood is a lifelong dream and you think your life will never feel complete without having a family of your own, then this is an issue that will surely have to be resolved at some point. This doesn't necessarily mean that you have to end your relationship; however, it isn't a topic you can just ignore in the hope that it will magically fix itself in time. You will need to discuss your feelings with your partner and work out a compromise. Maybe he isn't ready now, but he might be willing to start a family in a set period of time. Another compromise may be that whilst you will not be outright trying to have a baby, you may not want to do anything to prevent having one either. This informal approach could allow him to feel less anxious; sometimes letting fate decide can take the pressure off.

Despite your wants, you must remember to listen carefully to your partner and what he is saying. Don't misread the fact that he doesn't want or isn't ready for children as a sign that he doesn't love you or isn't committed to you. His feelings about whether he wishes to be a father are different from the feelings about you and the relationship.

However, if you are both committed to the relationship and want each other to be happy, then someone may have to make a sacrifice to make the other person happy.

Which roles will we take?

Sixty years ago deciding who would care for the child would not have been an issue: the father would go to work and the mother would stay at home, run the house, and raise the children. But times and the way we live our lives have changed. It is no longer unusual to find couples who split housework fifty-fifty, or stay-at-home dads who hold down the fort whilst their wives go back to work.

As the distribution of the workload is one of the biggest issues that new parents disagree about, it will be beneficial to discuss how you will divide the work for both the house and the children beforehand. Will the person who stays home be completely in charge of all things "family" during the work week, and the person who goes to work only helps out on weekends? Or will you divide the responsibilities equally? For example, does the stay-at-home parent have full responsibility for the house and children for the whole day, thereby allowing his or her partner to relax at night after a big day at work, or does the parent who works start chipping in as soon as he or she gets home?

And what about the night shifts? Who will be getting up in the middle of the night? Will it be just one of you or will you take turns? Are you willing to sleep in the spare room so your partner can get some rest? Or do you think that you both should share the sleepless nights equally?

Once you go back to work there are even more things to consider, like who will be in charge of picking up and dropping off the kids? What happens if you need to work overtime or travel for work? Will you both share the load or will only one of you have the responsibility? And what about discipline—will you play good cop/bad cop or both be equally in charge?

There are many decisions to make about your roles as parents, so working out the logistics in advance and agreeing on solutions that work for both of you can help you avoid the risk of one parent feeling frustrated and unhappy when he or she bears the brunt of the child-rearing responsibilities. Knowing who will do what means that your home will run more smoothly and your child will know what to expect from each of you.

Having a child is not just a lifetime commitment for you; it is a life partnership that requires equal effort from both sides. Committing to making a team effort will definitely help create a happier household.

Parenting styles

When the baby cries, do you go to him right away, or leave him for five minutes? When a child is "naughty", would you smack her, or explain that her actions are unacceptable and put her in the "time out" corner? These questions and thousands of others will be part of your daily life once you become parents. Even if you think you know your partner inside and out, there is nothing like a child to make you realise just how different you may be.

People often have unique and deep-seated views about child raising, most of which have been established during their own childhood and that generally determine how they think a child should be raised. One of the ways to reduce arguments is to have a few discussions about how you want to raise the kids beforehand so you can work towards getting your parenting styles in sync. Whilst as parents you may reach an agreement as each situation arises, you may also find that differing views on parenting open some very large cans of worms, so be prepared for some heated discussions along the way.

Will trying to conceive affect our sex life?

At first trying for a baby may seem like fun, and it might even be a blessing that you will be forced to find some time in your busy lives for your personal life. However, sometimes people worry that the technical side of baby making, such as timing intercourse, could mean the loss of all the spontaneity and excitement in their sex lives. And if you decide to increase your chances of conceiving by charting your cycle, then there will certainly be times when you will need to work hard to get in the mood.

Planning your love life by a clock or calendar can look a bit unromantic, but sometimes losing a bit of spontaneity can be more appealing than waiting another month, particularly if time is not on your side. If you are concerned about losing the fire in your love life, then the best way to overcome this is to have both intimate times aimed at conceiving and intimate times that are just for you, and just for fun with no pressure.

Will it affect our relationship?

Once you become parents, the dynamics of your relationship will change. Where you may have once lived in perfect harmony, often your new roles will see divisions and new lines drawn as your priorities change and you adjust to your new life as a family. There is no other way to put it: a baby will affect your relationship in a really big way! No longer will you be two different people who share their lives together, but rather you will be Mum, Dad, and baby, and the quality time you enjoyed as a couple will be a thing of the past … at least for a while.

Life as a new mother is busy and all consuming, and sometimes a woman's changing priorities can have an adverse effect on the relationship. Husbands may feel neglected and resentful when they realise they are no longer the dominant person in their wife's life. Add to this sleep deprivation and constant crying and even the most perfect union will begin to feel the strain.

The pressures of raising a young child are quite significant and can often magnify what used to annoy you about each other tenfold, leading to tension and bickering. It won't be your fault or his or even the baby's, but is something you will have to accept as a realistic part of bringing a new baby home.

Couples will find that trying to undertake significant lifestyle changes at a time when they are getting less sleep, and have fewer opportunities to be together, will mean they have less patience with things that didn't seem to bother them before. New parents can find themselves taking their exhaustion and frustration out on each other, and even the most harmonious and well-adjusted couples could find themselves arguing for the first time in their lives.

Most couples will survive the disruptions of their child's first years, but keeping your relationship alive is important during this time and will require consistent effort on both sides. The key to a long-lasting relationship will be finding ways to keep re-con-necting with each other even though your lives are fuller than ever before.

When considering how a child will affect your relationship, you need to think about how much one-on-one time you are prepared to give up, what your feelings are on personal space and alone time, and how you will achieve a work/life balance. Accepting that you will be sharing your life and your partner with someone else and that sometimes the relationship will have to take a back seat is an essential prerequisite to becoming a mother.

Women also worry about how a child will affect how their partner sees them. Will a baby ruin the passion and affection they now share with their partner? Will their partner still find them attractive after watching them give birth? Will they still be sexy after pregnancy has changed their bodies? Many women are body conscious or already concerned about keeping the spark going in their relationship, so these kinds of questions are valid concerns.

It is essential for your partner to know beforehand that your body and the structure of your relationship will change. Both of you will need to understand that the intimacy and spontaneity in your love life will vary but that it won't be like that forever. And remember that baby's usually only increase the feelings couples have for each other. So, when the time comes to bring out your old, abandoned lingerie, be assured the last thing on your partner's mind will be the delivery suite; instead, he will be looking at you as the wondrous creature who brought him the miracle of his own child.

Financial Concerns

It may not be the most romantic subject to talk about, but working out whether you have the means to raise a child is an important part of the decision-making process. Luckily, it's also the easiest determining factor to figure out since once you do the sums, you'll know whether you will or won't be able to provide for a baby.

Try not to get too bogged down with worrying about future expenses like braces, private school fees and your teenager's latest technological must-have. Raising children is expensive, but they start out reasonably cheap, and there will be plenty of time for your personal circumstances to change and improve as your child grows. Still, knowing that you will be financially stable going into parenthood and that the bills will get paid on time will allow you to relax and concentrate on raising your child.

What does it really cost to have a baby?

In 2013, the AMP.NATSEM Income and Wealth Report estimated that it would cost the average middle-income family around $812,000 to raise two children from birth until around the age of twenty-four. Whilst you will never be able to put a price on the pleasure your children will bring you, it is a considerable investment for something you may not be sure you want.

What are the some of the costs associated with having a baby?

Pregnancy, including medical tests, obstetrician, and new clothes

Increase in private health insurance costs

Labour, including the hospital, anaesthetist, and paediatrician

Setting up for the baby, baby goods, clothes, equipment, toys, and so on

Ongoing child medical costs and specialist appointments

Ongoing child costs including clothes, nappies, and cleaning products

Extra groceries, beginning with formula and speciality baby foods

Loss of earnings whilst you are on maternity leave

Activities like playgroup and swimming lessons

Childcare

Loss of income if you only return to work part-time

Increase in water, telephone, and energy costs.

As your child grows, there will be other costs to consider:

School fees, uniforms, camps, equipment, and fundraisers

After-school activities like sports, music, and swimming

After-school and vacation childcare

Medical expenses, including dental and orthodontic work

Clothes, toys, furniture, and technological equipment like computers and phones

Additional costs for holidays, hotels, and travel

Parties, both their own and all the presents for friends

Pocket money

And when you think they are almost off your hands, there's still more:

TAFE or University costs

Cars

Moving out of home

Weddings

Grandchildren

And let's not forget ...

"Mum, Dad, can you lend me some money?"

What medical costs are involved with having a baby?

How much a pregnancy will cost will depend on where you live and if you want to go through a private or public health care system. In Australia, the Medicare system will cover most of your out-of-pocket expenses for public hospitals and even GP visits, whilst private care, even with the top private health insurance, will turn into quite an expensive enterprise.

Some of your expenses will include specialist appointments, ultrasounds, and blood tests, as well as heartburn tablets, pregnancy vitamins, stretch mark creams, and maternity clothes. Once the baby is born, your hand will still be in your pocket to pay for in-house hospital costs such as anaesthetist, pathology, pharmacy, and paediatrician fees, and ongoing specialist fees for your post-natal check-ups.

As your pregnancy progresses, appointments and tests become more frequent, and it does begin to add up. If you live in Australia, you can probably expect around thirty-five per cent of these costs back on Medicare, and up to around eighty per cent once you reach the Australian Tax Office's Medical threshold.

I went through my pregnancy with top health insurance coverage and still managed to pay around $4,500 (approximately $2,500 after rebates), and this was for a straightforward pregnancy and birth. If you have complications in your pregnancy, get sick or require specialist assistance, hospitalisation, or genetic testing, or specialist postnatal care for your baby, your costs could be much higher. When you take into consideration all of your medical expenses as well as the costs of purchasing maternity and nursing clothes, you could be looking at a total of about $5000 up front, and you haven't even spent a cent on the baby or the nursery yet!

What are the basic set-up costs?

Providing for a child doesn't come cheap, but calculating your basic set-up costs doesn't have to be difficult. To get started, try breaking things down into nursery basics, wish list items, and ongoing costs for the first year, like nappies, wipes, and clothing.

For a first baby there is a lot to purchase, and you will have all sorts of expenses from a cot to a car seat to clothes and nappy cream. If you are buying everything from scratch, you could be looking at anything up to $5,000 to set up your nursery and pay for all the clothes, equipment, and toys you will need for the first year.

Luckily, you will probably get a lot of your starter items at your baby shower if you have one, and can sometimes set up a gift register at a store for big-ticket items. You will probably also get a few hand-me-downs. Once I announced my pregnancy, everyone from my best friend to the girl at work to the next-door neighbour clamoured to pass on all kinds of beautiful pre-loved baby goods.

If you do need to shop for additional items, then the best way to deck out any nursery is to beg and borrow what you can, buy online for second-hand goods, and watch out for the big department store sales throughout the year. If you are savvy, you can save thousands.

Educational costs

Everyone wants the best for their children and their future, and with free education now a thing of the past even in public schools, you will want to think about how much it will cost to educate your child, and factor this into your long-term financial and return-to-work plans.

It may be five years before your child starts prep, but their education and care costs could begin around their first birthday since expenses often begin with social activities like playgroup or swimming lessons. Once you return to work, costs will include ongoing childcare fees, which as of 2015 stand at around $70.00 to $100.00 AU per day, subject to childcare rebates.

After a few years of day-care, your child will enter mainstream education. At this point, you will have the option of public or private schooling. A private education will set you back anywhere from $1,000 to $7,000 per semester, though you will incur some expenses regardless of your choice of schools. These include ongoing costs such as uniforms, sports and music equipment, stationery, books, excursions, camps, fundraising, and school contributions. Other expenses may include private tuition and before- and after-school care. Once your child's mandatory education is completed, your ongoing costs could continue if you choose to help your child pursue further education such as TAFE or University.

There is no denying that educating a child is expensive, and you certainly cannot put a price on a good education. Yet it is still important not to worry too much about these costs when you first decide to have a child. If providing an excellent education for your child is important, then the best way to plan for the future is to create a scholarship fund or open a bank account whilst your child is still in nappies.

Less income, more expenses

Up until now you have been enjoying the no-expenses-spared life of a D.I.N.K (Double Income No Kids), but once you become a mother, you will very quickly move to the new life of a penny-pinching S.I.N.K (Single Income Nice Kids). Once you decide to have a family, not only will you lose or reduce your income whilst on maternity leave—or permanently if you can afford to go back to work part-time or not at all—but your weekly costs will increase.

When budgeting time rolls around, couples will often focus primarily on the actual income lost during planned leave; however, when it comes to making long-term financial plans, it pays to have a contingency in case you get sick or there are complications that force you to leave work earlier than expected.

To work out a budget that incorporates the additional costs of raising a child, try starting with the minimum amount of money you can survive on, and then adding extras for ongoing costs and emergencies. Spend some time looking at a few variations, taking into account various factors such as the difference between staying home and working part- or full-time. As a parent, it pays to know how flexible your financial situation is, as you can sometimes earn the same amount in three days as you do in five simply because of the reduction in tax and the inclusion of social service and other family benefits.

Practical Concerns

Your home

You may look at your current home and think, *home sweet home*, but if you decide to have children, you will need to evaluate whether your current abode is suitable for a baby. Do you have enough room for a new addition? Is your current location suited to a baby? Are you in a place in which you would like to bring up a child?

At the moment, your inner-city pad may be perfect as it is a mere five-minute stagger from your favourite night club; however, it may not be the calm and peaceful retreat you will want when you are trying to keep a sleeping baby asleep.

Having cappuccinos available at your doorstep is great now, but what about in the years ahead when your child becomes a toddler? Stairs, balconies, and lots of plain glass window panels won't necessarily make the safest or most practical environment for a curious two-year-old, not to mention the extra effort required to drag prams, nappy bags, and a port-a-cot up three flights of stairs.

If after evaluating your current home you decide that you may want to move house, then consider the financial costs and the practicalities of when to make the shift. Are you able to sell your property now and move before getting pregnant? Or would you wait until the impending growth of your family before searching for greener pastures? If you do wait until you are expecting, consider the physical and emotional burdens and stresses of trying to move houses whilst pregnant.

If you are lucky enough to be able to stay put, then you need only look at what needs to be done to turn your current crash pad into a family home. Time can get away from you when you are pregnant, and you certainly don't want to end up like one of those wives on a lifestyle show who finds herself heavily pregnant and knee-deep in sawdust whilst her frazzled husband promises that it will all be done before the baby arrives.

Before throwing away your contraception, have a think about what your needs and wants are versus your family budget. If you do need to renovate or sell your trendy two-bedroom apartment for a family home, first take the time to assess whether you are able to afford the new higher mortgage or rental rates on one income and with an increase in your weekly living costs. It is also worth considering whether buying the perfect long-term family home now may help you avoid the hassle of moving again if your family continues to grow.

Transport

Another thing to think about when considering finances is transport. If you are currently a one-car family or rely on public transportation, think about how you will get around once the baby is born, particularly how you will work childcare pick-ups and drop-offs once they become part of your daily routine.

Even if you already own one or more vehicles, consider whether they are suited to a couple of kids. Once you have children, your car will become an extension of your house and will be filled with baby essentials like a pram, nappy bag, and toys. Your small run-around might suit you now, but once your baby arrives you may find there is little room for shopping or luggage, so investing in a family-friendly design could be useful.

Your career

Your career is usually a big part of your life before having children, and whether you are employed as a retail assistant, a pole dancer, or a neurosurgeon, most women will have the same fears and questions about how a baby will affect their jobs.

Many women start their working lives thinking that when the time is right they will find a way to balance career and family. As time goes by, however, women often find that their plans change due to time and circumstances: they "get busy", their careers blossom, and children become less of a priority.

Whilst most working women can probably relate to this situation, it seems to be even more prevalent for high-powered corporate women. The fairer sex may be finally breaking through the glass ceiling, but it's coming at a cost, with research showing that around half of all career women do not have children. It is these same women who are having the hardest time deciding whether to continue their careers without interruption and risk the disappointment of not having children, or to take time out for motherhood and risk hijacking their chances of career progression.

Before you set out on the path towards the dual role of a working mother, consider how a child will fit in with your career. If you work nights and weekends or have to travel on short notice, then you will have to be even more organised than the average mother. And to do both, you will either need a supportive husband or a flexible nanny. Also, consider whether you have a job that you would be more than happy to ditch or if you are in your dream role after years of climbing the corporate ladder. Think about the real costs of putting your career on hold, and I don't mean just the financial aspects. Will being out of the loop for a few years make you lose your edge, miss out on promotions, or put you out of a job altogether? And if it does, do you care?

If you think taking time off might have a detrimental effect on your career, perhaps consider moving into a more "child-friendly" line of work beforehand. This may be a straightforward step with your current skills and experience, or you may need further training to take on a new role. If, on the other hand, you are self-employed or in a profession that wouldn't allow you to change jobs or take a year off, then things could be a little more difficult, but not impossible, since that's where quality childcare and family support comes in.

Unfortunately in some cases, your career will suffer even if you keep your skills up and return to the same occupation. Depending on the type of industry you are in, you may find that things have changed whilst you were away, business contacts have grow cold, and the memory of all your earlier hard work and achievements has been forgotten. Other colleagues may even think you should go to the back of the line and prove yourself all over again. Often when a woman returns to work she has to work a little harder to reach that next promotion or simply to restore her old reputation.

This unfair but realistic view of the corporate world is why so many professional women worry they can't have it all and choose to delay starting a family. But as frightening as the risks might seem, all workplaces and situations are different, so if your job is valuable to you and you still genuinely want to have a family, look a little deeper into the options available to help you achieve both.

Perhaps you will need to consider taking less time off work or doing some part-time consultation work from home whilst on maternity leave. To give you a chance to focus more on your career, perhaps your partner could rearrange his work responsibilities or work fewer hours to care for the baby. Or maybe you could enlist the help of your parents or look into hiring extra help with either the baby or the housework. There are always options and ways to make things work. It is just a matter of thinking about how you will combine career with family and working out what is more valuable to you.

Once you are pregnant, it will help if you are in a job that is supportive of pregnant women since you will need some flexibility in your work hours, particularly when you are just too sick to work or are so uncomfortable you want to leave early. You also need an understanding boss when it comes to taking time off to attend doctor and specialist appointments.

Check into your company's policy on maternity leave, carer's leave, and procedures for returning to work. If your employer doesn't offer maternity benefits or flexible work arrangements, it may be worth changing jobs and finding a company that is more supportive of families.

Work versus staying home

Most parents have two full-time jobs: the one they do for their employer, and the other, which is raising their kids. Trying to juggle the demands of work and family can be tough, and finding the right balance between the two can be tricky.

Women who are fortunate enough to be able to throw themselves into the challenging but joyful job of being a career mum are usually happy to give up their full-time positions to spend more time with their children. In some cases, though, women who are used to earning their own income may not feel entirely comfortable relying wholly on their husband's wage and may like the idea of having something just for themselves. Often women will look towards gaining some kind of financial independence through such avenues as part-time work or home-based businesses.

When deciding whether to be a working mother or a stay-at-home mum, think about if you would be happy being home every day, or if you would need the challenge of work and some adult socialisation to keep you stimulated. Women used to a fast-paced business life may find the early days of raising a child boring, and can feel like they are on a short leash trapped between naps, feeds, and endless housework. Others find—sometimes in spite of themselves—that running a home and caring for a child full-time is all the stimulation they want and is more enjoyable than they ever imagined, particularly, if they have already dedicated themselves to the workforce for the past twenty years or so.

Whatever your choice, it will need to be one that works for you and your partner and your children, and one that fits your financial situation and life goals. Just remember that having a baby adds a second shift to the end of your working day, so looking at your options and trying to work towards a goal of some work/life balance will be beneficial to the whole family.

Life as a working mum

Just about the time you are getting used to being home with your baby, a routine check of your diary shows your maternity leave is coming to an end. Whilst you may be looking forward to declaring, "You're not the only one who has to work tomorrow", when your husband moans that the baby is awake again, most women will experience mixed emotions about returning to work, and some will find the transition easier than others. Whether you are returning to work by choice or by necessity, there will be a few challenges to overcome: first, securing good, reliable, and affordable childcare; second, dealing with the stress and guilt of leaving your child in someone else's hands; and third, adjusting to a life that now holds dual responsibilities.

No matter how well you knew your job before you went away or how easily you fall back into your previous role, rejoining the workforce is not easy. There will be the obvious expectation that you will perform well on the job no matter what is happening in your personal life, except now instead of going home to collapse on the couch after a gruelling day, you will have the responsibility of looking after a child. Not only will you need to take care of your child's basic needs like food and sleep, but you will need to ensure you spend quality time with him or her at night and on the weekends. Being a career mum is exhausting and time-consuming, and it leaves little time for personal activities and relaxation.

In the early days, you may also feel conflicted when your professional life is always interrupted by illness, sleepless nights, and must-attend preschool activities, or conversely when you have to put your job before your child. Most mums will tell you they feel guilty when work affects their family life, and guilty when their family life affects their work. It is a struggle.

Whilst most women do find a way to make a success of it, quite a few women, me included, have considered throwing in their jobs simply because it seems too hard. I have certainly had days when I have been embarrassed about calling in sick again, and days when the guilt about being away from my child is overwhelming. Although many mums experience the back-to-work blues at some point, the reality is that a high percentage of mothers from varying professions do work and do manage to get by. In fact, a 2013 family trends report published by the Australian Institute of Family Studies shows that in 2011 around 65% of mothers were in paid employment, proving that a working mother is by no means a new phenomenon.

If you do decide to go back to work after having a baby, you will find that whilst it will be difficult to juggle both roles in the beginning, you will eventually establish a routine and your child will settle into childcare and your new busy life. Before having a child, the idea, of getting up at 6 am after being up with a baby half the night, may seem impossible, but over time you do learn to adjust and balance both roles. It is a matter of setting priorities, being organised, and resting when you can—and friends promise me that it does get easier as your children get older.

Chapter 8

Pre- and Post- Baby Considerations

Once the decision has been made to start a family, everything in your life will change: the way you work, live, and play will be affected by a little person you haven't even met yet. Let's take a look at some of these changes in more depth.

Diet

Choosing to have a child will mean making some changes to your diet. These changes will need to be made from the moment you commence your pre-conception care until you wean your baby.

Most of us are aware of the obvious don'ts, such as smoking, coffee, and alcohol. However, many aren't aware of some of the other no-nos such as soft cheeses, sushi, pre-made salads, and deli meats. Once pregnant, you will need to watch everything that goes into your mouth, including prescription and over-the-counter medicines.

Now that we as a society have a better understanding of how the health of the mother affects the long-term health of her child, and realise the importance of feeding our bodies well through good nutrition and daily supplementation, most mums-to-be will want to make a conscious effort to feed their baby bump well every day.

Your body

Body image is a major concern for most women, and after a lifetime of over-eating, under-eating, hiding under enormous t-shirts, and doing all sorts of unhealthy things to stay skinny, losing control of your body can be a scary proposition. Many women will confess to feeling petrified at the thought of putting on weight and losing their shape during pregnancy, so much so that we now have an emerging new eating disorder known as Pregorexia, the following of extremely low-calorie diets in order to stay slim during pregnancy. Which is clearly a dangerous practice for both mother and baby.

Unfortunately, the media have not helped the fairer sex's habit of body bashing. Thanks to modern journalism, even the creation of life is no longer held sacred. There is a new culture of unrealistic expectations put on women as we are bombarded with amazing celebrity post-baby transformations, suggesting that not only is it possible for us to bounce back to our old selves in a matter of weeks, but that our bodies will be the same if not better than ever before.

Sure, it's nice to daydream about getting the same results, but in the real world we know this is just another ploy by the tabloids to sell magazines. Most of us are just ordinary people who don't have access to personal trainers, chefs, nannies, and a photographer to airbrush our post-baby photos. We are mortal women who will have to learn to live with our new bodies.

Creating a life is a miraculous thing, and our body needs to undergo significant changes during its nine-month journey, some of which will be temporary and others permanent. New mothers will be given a variety of reminders of their baby's arrival, from stretch marks to pigmentation to the deflated balloon that hijacks the space where their stomach used to be. Fortunately, and despite our fears, some women will be able to push aside their insecurities and see their changing shape as a blessing but for others, the experience will be difficult, leaving them worrying whether their bodies will ever be the same again.

It is impossible to know how pregnancy will affect your body since everyone is different, but any mother will tell you that her body has never been the same again since she had children. Most find they have been left with a more rounded, voluptuous body, which may include curvier hips and waist, whilst others notice changes in their shoe size or hair colour. Luckily, though, the life of a new mother is so busy she will have little time to worry about how she looks.

Just remember that your body was designed to be pregnant. If you need to bury any inner demons about body image, now is the time to do it. Think about the big picture: not only will relaxing through your pregnancy make you a healthier and happier mum, but you will also finally have an excuse to let your stomach out after lunch. It's true that you may never have the body back that you have now, and you might lose your six pack, but thanks to hours of nursing and carrying your baby, you can look forward to gorgeous arms and shoulders and the knowledge that you will look fantastic in your strapless summer dresses.

Your appearance

The first few months with your baby will be a very busy time. There will be a lot to learn and do, so much so that you will find precious little time to invest in your personal appearance. It won't matter how good your child is or how organised you are, there will be days when you are still wearing pyjamas at four in the afternoon. And it won't be just occasionally; it will be a *lot* of the time.

Eating up a day is what babies do best, and most new mums find that basic grooming is one of the first things they let go. Simple things like shaving their legs, painting their toenails, or blow drying their hair often become luxury items on a wish list rather than a regular part of their daily lives. In the early days, forget about matching underwear: it will be about ponytails and matching shoes. If you are a regular at the day spa, then you will soon find that brushing your teeth and slipping into a fresh change of clothes can be almost as good.

And unless you have an easy baby and a good babysitter, you will need to rethink high-maintenance hairdos since getting weekly trims and having your roots done will most likely become a thing of the past. When I think back to the days when I would not leave the house without a flick of mascara and splash of lip gloss, I find it amusing that I am now satisfied if I remember to change out of my slippers.

Lifestyle

Your life *will* totally change, and you *will* become a different kind of person once your child is born. I have to admire women who say or think that a child won't change anything, because having a baby changes everything! It changes the way you think, the way you dress, the way you eat, the way you talk, and the biggest one of all, the way you sleep! Understanding that the changes in your life will be dramatic can help you avoid a nervous breakdown later on, and the quicker you learn to accept that there will be significant changes, the easier life will be.

Most women probably consider the significant and visible lifestyle changes like not going to concerts or saying goodbye to the club scene, but what many may not realise is that having a baby affects every single part of your life and how you live it. It also affects your home life on many levels. Just think: no swearing, no smoking, no parties, and definitely no more sleep-ins. You won't even be able to rely on simple things like privacy in the toilet.

With a child around you will have to accept your home, is no longer going to be just your own. Favourite ornaments will be packed away as you learn to share your space with all their bits and pieces—highchairs, bouncers, and toys everywhere! And once you have adjusted to life with a baby, expect the intrusions to continue. First friends will be stopping by for milk and cookies, and later, loud and unruly teenagers will treat your home as a drop-in centre. Once you become a parent, your life is never going to be the same again!

Social life

Your social life will undergo a readjustment from the moment you fall pregnant. At first morning sickness will be the reason you miss certain events and activities, and later you will feel too fat, too tired, and simply not that interested in going out. Once you are trying to grow a little human being, most of your old, noisy, and over-crowded hangouts will not be the places you want to be. It is important to realise early that there will be a decrease in the types of events and social activities that you can attend. Whatever your social life looked like before, expect change and understand that it may never return to what it was.

After the baby is born, your social life will be affected by interrupted schedules and lack of sleep. Babies are pretty portable when they are small, but even so, social engagements may seem like such a hassle that you may prefer to stay at home with your new little bundle. Then after twelve months of living by a feeding and sleeping schedule, you will be craving company and entertainment, and your girlfriend's latest invitation will seem like a fun opportunity to get some of your old life back. But if it is not a bub-friendly event, you may not enjoy it as much as you once may have, and it is often easier and more enjoyable to find activities that suit the whole family.

These are the choices that new mums make, and the reason that a lot of women think you become boring and less vivacious once you become a mother. But what actually happens is you just become a bit more responsible, and what you begin to see as fun, your childless friends see as less entertaining—aka *boring*! It's not that you enjoy life any less; rather, you enjoy it in different ways, and a lot of the time the fun is had at home behind closed doors.

Children can add a whole new dimension of fun and laughter to your life. We often lose our sense of excitement and wonder as we age, and whilst the hustle and bustle of life with children can be a bit restrictive and can drive you slightly mad, it is at the same time invigorating. Once you become a mother, you will only remember your house as this big, quiet space and will wonder what you used to do with all your time.

Despite my reassurances, you may be worried that a baby will ruin your social life completely but it really comes down to how you approach it. I know some mums who are "Nap Nazis"—it doesn't matter what they are doing or how much their children are enjoying themselves, at nap time, the fun stops and they go home. By choosing to live by a rigid schedule, their social lives are obviously going to be affected quite a bit.

Some people like routines and, yes, routine is necessary for helping a child feel safe and secure. That said, my husband and I are more open to bending our routine to live in the moment and have tried to be more flexible in our child raising. Of course, we have some restrictions around what we do and when we do things, however, we made a conscious effort to include Paige in our lives. She went dancing at her first blues festival at age two and a half, she loves and looks forward to our annual trip to the Buddha Festival, and she has already seen a couple of New Year's Eve firework displays. It *is* possible to have children and a social life!

Also, remember that having children doesn't mean you will never see another stamp in your passport. Friends of mine took their three-month-old to Sweden to meet her grandparents, and a neighbour went backpacking in New Zealand with her two-year-old son. It may take some time before you can return to all your old interests, but having children can also open up a whole new range of social activities. In some cases, it may even breathe new life into a somewhat stagnant existence. Women who are workaholics and who prefer to laze around at home after a big week at work may find that their social lives grow by having children.

Whilst overall the essence of your life and your interests don't change, the way you live your life—its rhythm—definitely does change. Since my daughter came along, I have found my social life is very different from what it was. I spend my spare time doing things that we can all enjoy or that make her happy. By default, many of my old friends and former activities have begun to fade away, but in return I have made new friends with similar interests and lifestyle restrictions.

My life has also changed from nights to days. Whereas once I would go out late, stay out late, sleep in, and have brunch around eleven, I am now one of those people who meet friends for breakfast. You know those energetic and bright-faced people you see at 7 am as you stumble by doing the walk of shame? Yes, believe it or not, if you want to have children, you will become one of those people too. I admit that this particular change is still quite a shock to my system! As much as I have adjusted to my new family life, every time I see a new festival or concert advertised, a wave of nostalgia flows through me as I shed a little tear and mourn my old life. As sad as it is to sometimes think about all the things I am missing out on, the moping is usually short-lived. In fact, most of the time, I will have forgotten all about it a few minutes later thanks to my little princess distracting me by jumping on my knee with a request for a story or a tickle.

Becoming a mum will mean moving into a new stage of your life, and will make a few dents in your social calendar. But don't worry! As your kids grow and begin doing their own thing, you will start reclaiming some of your past life. Of course, by then you will be so used to having the kids around that you will miss that part of your life instead.

Freedom

When we talk about freedom in the context of having children, we often focus on the freedom lost by becoming a mother, whether this is the freedom to pursue one's career, to maintain a lifestyle that includes both flexibility and spontaneity, or just to pursue one's own interests. Most women believe that children will be a hindrance to achieving one's life goals and that all personal pursuits and freedom will be lost.

The funny thing about freedom is that we interpret it merely as the ability to go places and do things when we want, with minimal hassle, so a life that is less flexible and more restrictive is seen as a bad thing. And, even though the loss of freedom that comes with having a baby won't be permanent, most childless couples fear it so much that is becomes the primary reason they delay starting a family. Because personal freedom and the power to make decisions is an important part of life, and I do think it can affect people's everyday sense of happiness, it's easy to understand why the thought of losing it worries people so much.

Adapting to the fact that someone wants and needs you 24/7 is not easy. But what has surprised me the most about becoming a mum is that it hasn't been forgoing whims like popping out for dinner that I have missed the most, but rather the simple freedoms I used to take for granted and now mourn: things like being able to sleep when I am tired, go to the bathroom when I need to, eat a meal when I'm hungry, or have a shower upon rising. Whereas I used to think that getting a massage and spending the afternoon at the hairdresser's was a luxury, I am now overjoyed when I get to change my chipped nail polish and read a few pages of a magazine uninterrupted.

Overall, the hardest thing about becoming a mother is getting used to and realising that I can no longer just get up and go whenever I want ... that I have lost my spontaneity entirely. Now I need to think about nap times, feed times, and how long I can reasonably afford to stay out. All of a sudden, a last-minute decision to see a friend for coffee will require a substantial amount of planning and packing. It is doable, but once you become a parent you have to be prepared to lose some control over your life and how you live it.

Living with worry

Although pregnancy is a joyous occasion, you may be surprised to hear it is also a very frightening nine months during which you never stop worrying. I spent most of my pregnancy feeling anxious, and couldn't wait to see my baby safely in my arms.

Like all mums-to-be, I expected to be nervous about miscarriage during the first three months, but I wasn't prepared for the continuous daily fear I felt for my baby. If I didn't feel her kicking, or if I had a strange sensation anywhere in my body, I panicked. I worried when I read statistics relating to birth defects in my age group. Tests went from being a routine part of my pregnancy to another thing to dread. Hearing a doctor say, "I just want to check something out", is frightening and waiting for test results is unbearable!

Towards the end of my second trimester a couple of days passed during which I hadn't felt my baby move. The thought of losing her was horrific. I have never felt more scared or anxious in my life.

I had hoped that after she was born my poor heart would get a break. But once she was home, there was a whole new list of things to worry about. First it was SIDS, and I worried about that *all* the time. When my daughter slept longer than expected, I felt fear. There were nights when I would lie in my bed, too scared to move. I just knew that if I went into her room I would find her lying still, not breathing.

Once I got past my fear of cot death, it was meningococcal C. Then bullies! Then strangers! I felt like I was worried all the time. Even now when I look to the future, all I see is more anguish. Drugs! Violent crime! Teenage pregnancies! Will the fear ever go away? Probably not, but if I can stop my child from backpacking through Europe, dating, or getting married, I might sleep a little better.

I always knew parents worried, but never how much. In such a short space of time, I have come to realise that motherhood is all about love ... biting your nails and watching your hair turn grey. Sure, ninety-five per cent of what we worry about won't ever happen, but that won't stop us from pondering every horrible scenario when our child isn't home on time. From the moment you fall pregnant and every day after, be prepared to live in some sort of fear. Worry *will* become your new best friend.

Once you become a parent, you will finally understand why your mother yelled at you through a veil of tears when you came home late and forgot to call. And even though you had not ended up lying dead in a ditch as your mother had feared, once you have a babe in your arms, you will totally understand where she was coming from and may even feel a little sorry.

The hard yards

By now I am sure you've heard a hundred times how wonderful motherhood is, but have you heard about its trials and tribulations? About the tantrums and the tears? About the days when your mummy friends feel like pulling their hair out, or the nights they cry themselves to sleep from utter exhaustion? Yes, motherhood is an amazing experience, and the love you will feel for your child will be unsurpassable, but between all the joyous and happy moments, parents do experience a lot of stress and battle through a magnitude of daily obstacles and hardships.

Before becoming a mother, I was warned that having a baby would be hard—harder than anything I could imagine. Whilst I did believe what my friends and family were telling me, I honestly thought I would be okay. I knew my strengths and weaknesses and how to work through painful and challenging situations simply through sheer will and determination. I thought about all the hardships I had been through in my life and kept thinking, *I got through them, so I can get through this.*

But even though I was mentally prepared for the worst, I discovered that motherhood was, in fact, much harder than I had expected. I simply wasn't prepared for just how physically and emotionally exhausted I would be by the time my baby arrived, or how awful I would feel in the weeks post-delivery. I didn't realise how instantaneously motherhood arrives, and that there is no time to recover or ease into your new role. One minute I was dressing up for our last child-free date and the next I hadn't showered in days.

Despite everything I had been told beforehand, nothing prepared me for the ongoing frustrations, confusion, and feelings of inadequacy I would experience in the beginning. No one warned me about the really tough times, the times when I would feel entirely lost, lonely, and unable to go on. Nor did they mention the tears. There are so many of them, both yours and theirs, in the early days! So, whilst my aim isn't to put you off having a baby, it is to tell you the truth so you can go into this adventure with your eyes wide open and your tissues nearby.

Chapter 9

Fertility and Age

Before actively trying to fall pregnant, women think about their fertility about as often as their own mortality. But once the decision to have a baby has been made, they will need Mother Nature on their side to make their dreams a reality.

Women may all be genetically alike, but their journeys towards motherhood will differ. There are the lucky ones who will conceive the first time around, but most will find that it can take a while to fall pregnant. The important thing to remember is not to panic if it does not happen right away, since it is not necessarily a sign that there is something wrong. As our fertility declines with age—faster in women than in men—sometimes it is better to start a family sooner than later.

Fertility facts

Your eggs are with you from the time you are in utero. I find it amazing that when you are pregnant with your own daughter, you are also carrying the cells that will one day create your grandchildren, if your daughter decides to have children, of course.

We are physically able to conceive a child from quite a young age. Even though we are obviously much too young to be parents, it is possible to fall pregnant from as early as our first periods. Then the period of natural fertility can last all the way to menopause—and even beyond when considering the miracles of modern science. But, our most fertile time is during our early twenties, which is usually the time we are the least interested in motherhood.

When we are born we have approximately one million eggs, which reduce to around fifty thousand by age twenty and again to around fifteen thousand by age thirty-five. With each year that passes, our ability to conceive is further reduced.

In our twenties, we have around a thirty per cent chance of fertilisation each month; fifteen per cent in our early thirties; a mere ten per cent in our mid to late thirties; and a crippling five per cent once we reach our early to mid forties.

Another fact that is not widely known is that because an egg only lives for around twelve to twenty-four hours, women have a very small window each month in which to conceive. Whilst a single sperm may live for up to five days, most of its quality and energy is lost after about thirty-six hours. If you combine this with the fact that about only fifty of the millions of sperm released at ejaculation will reach the egg, then fertilisation no longer seems that easy.

Even if you are lucky enough to conceive, seventy per cent of potential pregnancies will end in miscarriage within a few days, thanks to the majority of fertilised eggs not living long enough to implant. These odds make falling and staying pregnant seem more miraculous than accidental, and are also the primary reason I recommend charting if you want to conceive quickly.

What affects fertility?

Whilst pregnancy is a natural part of life, it is not always easy to achieve and can be affected by many factors. A woman's age will definitely have an impact on her ability to get pregnant, as will well-known culprits such as alcohol, cigarettes, party drugs, and some over-the-counter medicines. As noted in previous chapters, other factors such as your weight, diet, and lifestyle can also affect your chances of conceiving.

The birds and bees talks we had at school may have suggested that falling pregnant was as easy as boy meets girl, but we are now starting to understand that many lifestyle and environmental factors can affect the health of your and your partner's reproductive systems. The more we learn, the more we come to realise that we need everything to be just right to conceive a healthy baby.

Aside from diet and lifestyle, there are a few things that you won't have control over: for you there are recognised medical conditions including blocked tubes, endometriosis, Polycystic Ovary Syndrome (PCOS) and hormone imbalance, whilst for him there is poor sperm quality/quantity.

Whilst many of these conditions can be treated medically, the treatments may be time-consuming, which can adversely effect your pregnancy timeline. If you suspect that you or your partner may have fertility issues, consult your doctor as soon as possible.

How does age affect fertility?

Age is the single biggest contributing factor relating to fertility issues. As we get older, fertility decreases for all of us due to the decline in quality and the increased chance of chromosome defects, in both eggs and sperm.

Women are born with a finite number of eggs, and whilst they may be out of sight, they are still the same age as you. So, it makes sense that the younger the egg, the healthier it will be, and the chances of it being damaged or having any abnormalities will be lessened.

Conception in older parents is also affected by women ovulating less frequently and men having a reduced sperm count. Men's declining fertility doesn't become a real issue until much later in life, whereas women will begin to be affected in their early thirties.

Another way in which age is a contributing factor in the reduction of fertility is that individual health conditions are more common in older women; for example, women over the age of thirty-five are more likely to have endometriosis or PCOS.

Not all older women will be affected by these issues; however, whilst doctors will encourage younger women to seek medical intervention if they have not conceived after twelve months, this time is halved for women in their mid thirties and beyond. Studies show that fertility issues are not uncommon and around one-third of all women between thirty-five and thirty-nine and about half of women forty or over, will experience some kind of problem. Research has also shown that it is highly unlikely for women over the age of forty-two to conceive a child with her own eggs.

Timing motherhood can certainly improve your overall mothering experience. However, if you do put off having children until later in life, there are a few more age-related matters to consider.

Miscarriage

One of the risks of waiting until you are older to have a baby is a dramatic increase in the likelihood of miscarriage. Whilst most miscarriages occur in the first trimester for women of all ages, the chance of losing a baby during this time increases with age. Studies suggest that, whilst the risk in your twenties is relatively small at around ten per cent, it rises to about thirty-five per cent for women aged thirty-five to thirty-nine, and continues to increase to around fifty per cent from age forty and over. Age-related miscarriage is mainly attributed to chromosomal abnormalities and has nothing to do with your health and fitness. It is simply a by-product of getting older, and is a sad but real part of the baby-making process.

Before you conceive, miscarriage is just a word, but once you have felt the excitement of a positive pregnancy test and have started dreaming of meeting your child, a loss can be devastating. No one can prepare you to deal with such a loss, and whilst the statistics may alarm you, don't let them deter you from your decision to have a baby. Remember that the chances of eventually delivering a healthy baby are high for most healthy women.

Increased risk of birth defects

As you get older, the risk of your child having a birth defect or disability increases dramatically. Whilst you will love your child no matter what, it is necessary to understand the added risk you take by delaying conception. A human embryo is susceptible to a multitude of genetic disorders and, as discussed earlier, the chance of a chromosomal birth defect increases as eggs age. The most common of these disorders is Down's syndrome. The research I have read suggests that the chances of your child being affected are 1 in 1,250 at age twenty-five compared to 1 in 100 at age forty. At the end of your first trimester, you can have a nuchal translucency scan, which will determine whether your child is affected by Down's or other disorders.

Coping with this kind of news would be extremely difficult for any parent-to-be and can happen to mothers of any age. But to minimise the risks, consider starting your family sooner than later.

Multiple births

Right now you may be struggling with the idea of one baby, but how would you feel about becoming a mother of two at the same time? Whether it is our body's last-ditch effort to make a baby or a way to get ready for menopause, for some reason as we get older our bodies can begin releasing two or more eggs during a cycle, thus increasing the possibility of conceiving multiple babies. Whilst many may say, "double the baby is double the fun", it can also cause double the trouble.

Multiple children could be a blessing for some, but for others could mean real hardship in terms of multiple workloads, multiple accommodations, and multiplied financial costs. If after considering all the statistics you think multiple births may be in your cards, it may be worthwhile to set up a contingency plan and budget to deal with that outcome, just in case.

Assisted fertility

Whether they have waited too long or due to an underlying medical condition, some women will need to undergo assisted fertility treatments to realise their dream of having a family. IVF (in vitro fertilisation) has indeed become popular over the last decade, mainly due to an increase in women having children later in life or on their own. Despite its popularity, remember that it is an expensive undertaking—physically, emotionally, and financially—that requires patience and perseverance.

If you have been considering IVF as your fall-back plan, proceed with caution and do your research. Average statistics show around a forty per cent success rate for a live birth in mothers under thirty-five, which drops down to around six per cent for women aged forty-one. Whilst IVF does boast success, it is not the magic bullet many people believe. The best way to approach this option is to seriously study your finances and decide whether you are willing and able to take the gamble.

Another aspect to consider is whether IVF will conflict with your cultural or religious beliefs. Although reproductive technology is fairly new, most major religions now have teachings and guidelines that will help couples understand how and what they can access in the world of assisted fertilisation. Fertility centres also help by providing speciality treatment plans acceptable to a range of faiths and situations.

Assisted labour

If you have always dreamed of a natural home birth, you may be disappointed to hear that older mums have an increased risk of labour complications. Unfortunately as we age, not only do our labours slow down but we become more susceptible to medical conditions such as high blood pressure, gestational diabetes, and placenta previa. These conditions increase the risk of stillborn and premature babies, which in turn increases the chances of forceps deliveries and emergency caesareans. With most doctors believing it too risky for older women to have babies at home, the longer you leave it, the greater the chances that you will need to have your baby in a hospital.

Time

Have you thought about how time will affect motherhood for you? Consider this: to have a baby you need to designate at least three months to pre-conception care, followed by up to another twelve months to fall pregnant, which could be extended by a miscarriage or the need for medical assistance. Now add nine months for the pregnancy itself, and you are looking at up to two years to have one child. If you want another, you will need to allow enough time for your body to recover before starting the whole process again. This could lead to a three- to five-year timeline to realise the dream of having two children

And if you start your family at age thirty-five, you will be in your sixties when your children are celebrating their milestone birthdays—and you could be celebrating a seventy-something birthday yourself by the time your first grandchild comes along. Obviously, the longer you delay, the older you will be at each stage of your child's life.

As an older parent, you will need to consider how children will affect future plans. Are you willing to put your life on hold to raise teenagers when you are in your fifties? And are you prepared to curb your spending and any significant travel plans until retirement?

Looking back, I now regret not starting my family earlier. When I look to the future, it saddens me that I won't get to spend as much time with my daughter as I would have been able to had I been younger when I had her. Most of us want our parents to be around for a long time to come, and as a parent it is awful thinking about not being there for your kids or being able to watch your grandchildren grow. If you think you might want kids, don't waste any more of your future time together and plan to have children sooner rather than later. Because once you become a parent, you will want to be around for as long as you can.

Motherhood over forty

The face of motherhood is changing. By choice, accident, or because they are in a new relationship, more and more women now have children later in life. These days some women are swapping a mid-life crisis for a mid-life pregnancy.

Thirty may still be the most common time to have children, but despite the previous section, there are certainly many benefits to pushing motherhood into your forties, including being more financially secure, being older and wiser, and simply knowing what you want out of life. Older mums also tend to have more patience, are more compassionate and are usually a lot more tolerant than they were in their thirties. Having had the time to invest in themselves, they are also generally better educated and a whole lot worldlier than they were in their youth.

Although we are becoming more comfortable with forty replacing twenty as the new age for first-time mothers, it hasn't stopped the negative press warning us constantly about the dangers of delaying motherhood. No one denies that maternal age is a significant risk factor when considering obstetric health, but we must also understand that plenty of forty-somethings have normal, healthy, and safe pregnancies and give birth to happy, healthy, normal babies every day. In fact, around four per cent of all births each year are accredited to women over forty.

Even if these statistics do give you some comfort, you may still be wondering whether you have the physical strength and stamina required to carry a child through nine months of pregnancy and beyond. When it comes to being a mum, a woman's heath is certainly more important than her age. An active forty-year-old woman who looks after her diet and leads a healthy lifestyle is more likely to have a less complicated pregnancy and birth than an inactive, overweight woman half her age who leads an unhealthy way of life. Once your child is mobile, you will yearn for the energy you had in your youth, but the truth is that having young children can often make you feel more invigorated and more interested in improving and holding onto your health and fitness than ever before.

Another issue that may bother some is how you may be perceived in society as an older mum, and whether you could be mistaken for your own child's grandparent. Yes, this could happen, and the only question you need to consider is whether it really matters. For years, fifty-year-old men have been dating twenty-three-year-old women, and they haven't stopped doing so just because people might mistake their girlfriends for their daughters. They do it because it makes them happy regardless of what other people think. The desire to have a child is no different at forty-one than it is at twenty-seven, and the marvellous thing about reaching your forties is that you are usually a lot more comfortable in your own skin and care a lot less about other people's opinions of your personal choices.

Also, consider how having a child later in life may affect you emotionally. When you have been child-free for so long, it's natural you would be set in your ways. You will need to evaluate whether you will be able to be more flexible and make the compromises required to become a parent.

On a final note, as a member of the "sandwich generation" you may want to consider how you might survive if you are caught between balancing the care of your children with the care of your aging or ailing parents. Many couples look to their parents as helpers and even possible guardians of their children should the need arise, but if you begin your family in your forties you may need to look further afield for that kind of assistance.

Of course, there are negatives and positives to having a baby later in life. The important thing is that you and your partner build your decision on what is going to give you pleasure both now and in the future.

Being child-free later on

Deciding whether to share your life with children is a personal choice. Motherhood is a wondrous journey of self-discovery though it is no secret that it can also be difficult, expensive, and time-consuming. It is certainly not for everyone. Whilst many women will make a decision to have a family, others will prefer to dedicate their lives to other pursuits or passions, be that their career, travel or other hobbies. These women realise they are already perfectly happy and that their lives are fulfilled. They don't feel the need to add anything or anyone else to the equation.

If you do decide to stay child-free, then you should congratulate yourself on being brave enough to be different from everyone else. It will not always be a smooth road. You will need courage to be strong in the face of social stigma and constant pressure from family and friends who are desperately trying to change your mind. Many people just don't understand that not everyone feels maternal, and you may forever be told that you will live to regret it, or will change your mind later on.

Sure as you mature and circumstances change; you may have moments of doubt; however, it may be preferable to experience feelings of doubt than to live with regret. It is normal for all people to look at their lives and reflect on decisions, and 'what ifs'. But if you do make this decision, then you need to realise that, at times, these feelings of doubt will arise.

At these times you will need to take stock of your life and remember all the benefits you have now because of your choice, such as, having time to spend with family and friends, as well as the time to nurture your personal relationships, hobbies and career aspirations. Not to mention the freedom, money and energy to spend some quality time on yourself, finding out who you genuinely are, and what you truly want out of life.

Whilst mothers will be desperately trying to fit their hobbies and interests in, and around their children, you will be open to pursue anything in this world that you like, without having to worry about toilet training, babysitting or teenage pregnancy along the way. You will have the freedom to be spontaneous, and truly let your hair down, to enjoy yourself without ever having to worry about the commitments of family life.

And if life is fun for you now, why do you think things will all of a sudden change just because you decide not to have a family? Sure there may be times later in life when your heart takes over, and you feel as you have missed out, but just remember it is always easy to pine for the choice that you didn't make. If you feel at some point as if there is a void in your life, then realise there are lots of ways to introduce children into your life to help fill it. They might not be your own, but a child's love is endless, and I am yet to find a parent who would knock back an extra set of hands or a babysitter for the weekend.

PART TWO

FROM CAREFREE TO MUM-Meeeee!

A personal journal

Chapter 10

From Carefree to Mum-Meeeee!

Creating a life – Thoughts from the human incubator

The thing I found most amusing about having a baby was that I practically had to die to let someone else live. Using a word like "die" may seem a strange way to describe the creation of life. But for me, pregnancy, birth, and the first months postpartum, whilst amazing, were also some of the most traumatic, emotional, and physically draining experiences of my life.

I am sure you have heard stories to the contrary from women who have told you how lovely pregnancy is, and how labour isn't that bad at all. But I must warn you: these women are the exception, not the rule. These are the women who I delicately like to describe as "the ones who have been kissed on the bum by a fairy". These lucky few are the ones who spread stories of inner joy, lightning-fast pregnancies, and forty-five minute labours. Their stories, whilst comforting to those still deciding, can lead childfree women into a somewhat false sense of security. Pregnancy and childbirth are certainly miraculous, but they are also tough, so when I hear these kinds of uplifting stories, I cannot help but think these women are either truly blessed or particularly good liars.

Yes, everyone's experience will be different, but it was this difference between perception and reality that prompted my desire to share my personal journey with others. Primarily, I wanted to share some real insight into what pregnancy can actually be like. I wanted other women to know not just about the aches and pains, but about the uncertainty, the fear, and the roller coaster of emotions you sometimes feel. I do not believe it is a good idea for women to make such a life-changing decision without all the information and without understanding what the whole journey *could* actually be like.

It became apparent to me throughout my journey that what I thought pregnancy would be like, what society portrays it as, and what it is really like are vastly different things. Of course, it can be fun being pregnant: you get lots of special attention, and it is amazing to feel life growing inside of you. But at the same time, it is also extremely trying and sometimes terribly lonely. No matter what anyone may say, pregnancy is a big deal! And being willing and able to undertake the task of carrying a baby for nine months is an essential part of the baby decision.

I sense that by telling my story, I may at times put you off having a baby altogether. But please remember that my pregnancy was unique to me. Whilst many women will have an equally hard or even more difficult time than I did, some will sail through pregnancy and step into motherhood as easily as slipping on an old pair of slippers. But I have always lived by the philosophy that if you expect the worst, then things can only get better from there.

I hope that by reading my story you may begin to understand what entering into motherhood can be like. That way, if you do decide to take the journey, you will be fully armed and mentally prepared for what may lie ahead.

So, grab a glass of Chardie whilst you still can and get ready to hear all about "the secret life" of a pregnant woman.

A PERSONAL JOURNAL

My last silly season

December

After two months of changing my mind every second day, by Christmas the decision has been made. The *will we regret it later?* question has won ... at least for now!

Despite the father-to-be being at peace with his decision, I still have some niggling doubts, probably due to the prospect of pregnancy and childbirth. Actually, I am quite jealous of Brad because no matter how much I try to convince myself, I am just not experiencing the same kind of confidence and certainty. To be perfectly honest, I am still so confused that I have secretly decided to delay making a definite choice for now. Instead, I am going to use the preconception care period as an opportunity for further reflection. *Perfect!*

With the decision made, (the decision not to make a decision, that is), and the pressure off, I will be able to relax over the coming months, knowing that if I do change my mind, nothing will be lost. I will have given my body a break from the pill, lost some weight, and improved my health, just like I promise to do every January. Easy!

January

I know it may seem a little bit premature but I am already worrying about getting my "pre-baby" body back. After a lifetime of struggling with weight and body image issues, the idea of giving up control over my body is scary, though quite funny at the same time. I mean, seriously, if I don't know whether or not I want to have a baby, then why am I so worried about what a pregnancy might do to my body?

Does it mean I have made up my mind?

Mid January

After a week of contemplating my post-baby body, I have started to wonder whether the body I have now is one I would like to get back … and after much deliberation I have decided that it isn't. So, to up the ante, I am going to add more exercise and better eating to my pre-baby plan. In fact, I am so serious about dropping a few kilos and getting healthy, I am making the ultimate sacrifice—I am going to cut back on alcohol.

With my nicotine addiction six years behind me, a golden ale or a glass or three of an aged vintage are now my only real vices. So this will be a true test of whether I am ready to start making some changes in my life, albeit under duress!

February

Well, this would have to be a first: it is February and I am still being good. This is surprising as my health kicks rarely last longer than a few weeks. I must admit I am pretty pleased with myself, but at the same time can't help but notice I am in complete denial about the reason I am making these changes to my lifestyle.

March

My mother grew up in the era of free love and shotgun weddings. So in my youth, she was prepared to give me a fair amount of freedom as long as I adhered to two pieces of non-negotiable advice. Do not take drugs, and do not get pregnant! I was pretty happy to heed to these warnings, which is why I think I am now having such a hard time coming to terms with the fact that I am willingly going to ignore her.

From the outside, making a decision seems so straightforward: all I need to say is, "Okay! Let's do it, let's try to have a baby." But I still don't feel ready. Even the idea, of having unprotected sex after twenty years on the pill, is absolutely terrifying! The action alone would mean that I was actually going to do it—try to get pregnant. My mind is spinning!

Meanwhile, on the other side of the parent-to-be camp, Brad is so excited he is counting down the days to conception. I am trying so hard to show the same enthusiasm, but still wake each morning with a mix of excitement and trepidation. I seem no closer to putting those niggling doubts to bed than I was three months ago!

April

Constant procrastinating has done nothing but make my head ache, so I have come up with a fantastic plan to alleviate the pain. I am going to delegate. My spare time will no longer be spent scribbling pros and cons on little yellow sticky notes, from now on, the onus is going to be on someone, or, in this case, something else. Yes! That's right. I am going to leave it all to chance. But this decision isn't going to be decided by the flip of a coin or the roll of the dice, I am leaving it in the hands of someone much more experienced... I am leaving it to Mother Nature and fate. Destiny can now vote whether motherhood is for me.

You may be a little shocked at this revelation, but I have had success with this approach in the past. Say, for example, I see a fantastic pair of boots on sale. I will usually pick them up and then use my trusty "meant to be" method: *Well, they truly are beautiful. But I probably can't afford them. However, if my size is still there on payday, then it was meant to be.*

You are probably scratching your head right now and thinking, "Surely this girl isn't putting the decision to have a baby in the same category as buying a new pair of boots?" The honest answer is both yes and no.

Most of you are probably familiar with the old cartoon portraying a demon and an angel sitting on opposing shoulders of some poor, confused soul. Well, in this case, the poor confused soul is me. With a constant battle between my mind and my heart, it feels as if there will never be a winning side. Even on the days I believe I am one hundred per cent confident in my decision, the little voices in my head start chipping away at my resolve. My feelings are similar to the famous "pre-wedding jitters", but, I am so sure I will never be satisfied with any decision I make that avoiding responsibility and leaving it all to chance seems like my only real option.

Fate, it is now up to you.

And so it begins.

April 13

It is morning, six-thirty-five am to be exact. The room is bright, suggesting a beautiful autumn day outside. The shadows which kept me company throughout the night are long gone. As I watch tiny strips of sunlight dance across the carpet it seems like any other day. Except, today is different! Today, I am throwing caution to the wind. Today I will begin my journey towards getting pregnant.

Attempting to be quiet, and not disturb the motionless form beside me, I reach towards my bedside table, in search of my new thermometer. I spent a few more dollars to get the digital kind, so all I have to do is pop it in my mouth and listen for a beep. As I wait for a reading, I lean back into my pillows and glance over at the father-to-be. He is slumbering peacefully. Watching his chest rise and fall, I can't help but feel my first pang of resentfulness at being the one who has to give birth. *Yes, you can sleep soundly*. I snarl softly. *You don't have to push something the size of a watermelon out of something the size of a grape.* Just the thought sends a shiver down my spine.

Suddenly, the silence is broken by the alarm clock blasting into action. Pumping out the latest chart stopper, the radio wakes Brad instantly. Upon opening his eyes, he looks my way, sees the thermometer, and smiles. Not wanting to spoil the moment, I push my negative thoughts away and smile back. We are going to be a family!

April 14

Here I am—day two. Filled with mixed emotions, I wonder what may be in store for me over the coming months. I am curious as to how long the process may take, or if it will be successful at all. I am both excited and scared at the same time. Just being off the pill still feels weird, after half my life on it! How long it will take for my body to regulate itself, I wonder. I just hope my natural rhythm hasn't been entirely ruined. The doctor says it could take up to eighteen months, but now that I have made up my mind I just don't think I could bear to wait that long. I hope something happens soon.

April 15

Closing the bedside drawer, I jump. There is a shadow at the door.

"Sorry didn't mean to scare you," Brad apologises quickly. "How are things going?"

"I don't know," I reply solemnly. "It has been seventy-five days and still no sign of Aunt Flo."

"Aunt who?"

"Oh." I smile. "Aunt Flo. It's just a nickname they use online to describe your period."

"Oh! Of course!" He laughs. "Well, I suppose it's out with B.F.F and in with A.F."

April 17

The weird thing, about trying to have a baby, is that your life suddenly starts revolving around a toilet. Instead of running in and out to have a quick pee, a trip to the loo suddenly becomes something to look forward to. Bodily functions become vogue. Finding out your aunt is coming to visit becomes exciting.

And today, after dozens of stealth trips to the office bathroom, I finally had a valid reason to run out of the cubicle yelling, "She's here, she's here!" It was only the realisation that my colleagues might think I had gone mad that reined me in. Instead, I celebrated my news by giving the air a little high punch instead.

April 21

I am feeling extremely nervous today. I am on a covert operation. I am going to use an OPK. This may sound like a weapon left over from Desert Storm, but it's actually just a harmless ovulation prediction kit I got on eBay and it promises to tell me when my little egg is coming.

After thoroughly checking the halls are clear, I set off for the bathroom. I have taken only a dozen steps when a familiar voice startles me. It's John, my best work friend.

"Hey, Immi, how are you doing?" Seeing he has my attention, he walks closer. "What did you get up to on the weekend?"

"Ahhh ... not much ..." I stammer. "Just a quiet one."

"That's not like you," he laughs. "Did you see the Eels Panthers game on Sunday?"

"Yeah ... sure," I mumble back, discreetly trying to slide my test kit up my sleeve.

"Well, how about that tackle from Hindmarsh?"

Normally, any conversation regarding my beloved Hindmarsh would be enough to keep me chatting for ten minutes, but I need an out. *What can I say? Oh, I know.*

"Sorry, got to pee. I'll catch up with you later."

Feeling as guilty as hell and sure he knows I am up to something, I fly into the bathroom and shut the cubicle door behind me. As I catch my breath and look around at the old seventies tiles, and wall full of graffiti, I wonder if this dingy bathroom will be the place where my life's greatest journey will begin.

April 26

I have spent most of this week, either bent over a sink dry-reaching or sitting at my desk watching the room spin. I am not sure where I contracted this nasty little stomach bug, but I suspect it is from one of the dozens of students that pass my window each day. I don't do sick very well, and if there is one thing in this world I hate more than tangled coat-hangers, it is nausea. So this morning as I splashed cold water on my face and contemplated a future filled with morning sickness, all I could think was, *maybe this whole baby thing is a bad idea, after all.*

April 27

I have been home for about twenty minutes, and during this time, I have done nothing more than stare into the fridge pouting. This is not a normal after-work practice for me, but I have a problem. You see, ovulation day is almost here, which means no wine for two solid weeks. This might not seem a big deal for some, but teetotalism isn't something I usually aspire to. To me, abstaining from something I usually class as a treat seems more punishment than precautionary measure. Accepting I am just too sick to have one last hurrah leaves me feeling deflated and short changed.

April 28

It is hard to say for sure, but this morning I thought I saw two very faint lines on my OPK. Normally when I look at the stick I see nothing. But today I was convinced something was there. To get a better look, I tried examining the results under a variety of lights. I try the fluro in my office, direct sunlight, and the light from my phone. But try as I might, I couldn't be positive whether I was holding evidence of luteinising hormone or a case of wishful thinking. I suppose only time will tell.

April 29

After yesterday's success—yes, I finally convinced myself something was there—my morning routine of peeing on a stick seems much less disagreeable. With the test strip in my hand, I sneak back to my desk in search of something with which to pass the required three minutes. Luckily, the flashing light of my desk phone provides the answer.

Hitting the retrieve button, I listen to the drone of unfamiliar voices. The first caller wants help identifying aggressive ants; the second hopes to stop tree frogs from singing. Only half listening, I am forced to replay the messages twice. The implication of a positive result fills me with such trepidation it is hard to focus on their words. For another sixty seconds I pretend not to look, but then my curiosity gets the best of me. Without realising it, I am out of my chair, and hovering over the bookshelf. My eye inadvertently catches a glimpse of colour. Squinting, I move closer.

Is that two pink lines? My heart skips a beat. *OMG! I think it is. And they are getting darker.* I grab the detection strip by the handle and hold it inches from my face. *OMG! Dark pink lines.* A squeal of delight escapes my lips. *The egg is coming!* Feeling self-conscious, I quickly look out my office window. *Wow! This is so exciting. I could actually conceive a baby this week.* Yesterday I desperately wanted to see pink, but today I can't believe it is real. Pleased, but frightened, I spend the next five hours, sitting at my desk, smiling and periodically checking that the lines are still pink.

April 30

I wake up full of bounce. Today is the Foo Fighters concert. I am super excited. I seem to be excited about everything these days. I am still a little nauseous and running a fever, but I don't care. Not only am I going to see one of my all time favourite bands but tonight will be an opportunity to experience what could be one of our last big nights out on the town. Go the Fooies!

I am packing for the hotel when Brad wanders into the bedroom.

"Babe, I think I have the flu!" he announces.

Oh great, I think, *not you too*. Undeterred, I try to make light of the situation. "Darl, it's the Fooies; we will just have a few bourbons and push through it!"

Attempting to muster some enthusiasm, he smiles. But his bravado is quickly replaced by a coughing fit. Patting his arm on my way to the bathroom, I don't dare mention that this could be "the week" and that he may require energy for more than just a concert.

11.15 pm

"Wow that was awesome!" Brad shouts over the applause.

"Yeah," I yell back. "I can't believe they played for three hours."

"And that we actually managed to stomach bourbon."

"Yeah, one drink each," I laugh back. "We've lost our touch!"

Following the crowd out of the auditorium, we look around for the sliver service car we booked earlier. As always the vehicle is right out front, and within minutes, we are seated comfortably heading towards town.

"So where you guys off to tonight?" Ash asks, looking over his shoulder. "Shall I drop you off near George Street?"

"Not tonight, bud," Brad replies. "It's back to the hotel for us."

Our driver laughs. "You guys sick or something?"

"Sure are," we reply in unison.

12.07 am

After waving goodbye to our chauffer, we catch the lift to our room. As soon as we are through the door, our shoes are off, and we change into more comfortable clothes.

"Wow, the view is fantastic," Brad says, wrapping a jacket around my shoulders.

"I know," I reply, stepping out onto the balcony. "I always love the city at night."

"So what now? Do you want to sit out here for a while?"

"Yeah sure," I say happily. "I've just got to do the Maybe Baby thingy first."

"No worries," Brad says. "I'll take my medicine whilst you're at it."

Not quite the memorable baby making experience I had envisaged.

"Well, don't keep me in suspense," Brad says, as I step out into the night.

"I've got partial ferns."

"Yes." He leans forward in his chair. "And what does that mean?"

"It means that you better hurry up and fill my glass, it might be the last red I have for a while."

May 1

For the first time ever, I wake up in a hotel bed without a hangover. Feeling good, I place my saliva sample on the window sill, and after testing the water, step into bliss. Letting the steaming H20 do its magic, I relax. I have always believed showers are more therapy than hygiene. When I finally turn off the taps and step out on the stark white tiles, I feel refreshed and rejuvenated.

Slipping into the complimentary bathrobe, I decide to see what fate has for us. Holding the small white microscope to my eye, I press the button. *Well, well, well, what do we have here?* As I look at the three enormous fern leaves in front of me, I feel Brad step into the shower cubicle behind me. *I hope you're feeling better today darling. Because, baby ... it is nearly time to dance.*

I know I should be ecstatic, about my impending ovulation, but instead I am just confused. My emotions are all over the place. Up until this exact second, I honestly believed I was ready, that I was finally at peace with my decision. But now that the time has arrived, my excitement is accompanied by a significant chunk of fear. I am absolutely terrified. My stomach is churning and instead of thoughts of romance, all I can think is, *oh no! I am going to have unprotected sex! I could get pregnant! What are you doing, you stupid crazy woman?*

As the day progresses, panic continues to dominate my senses. I try to calm myself down with thoughts of the obvious. *Come on, Imogen, relax. This is what you want.* But for all my convincing and pep talks, the fear does not subside. As much as I try to muster some enthusiasm for a possible conception, I can't help but feel that something is terribly wrong. It feels that by attempting to get pregnant, I am going completely against the grain of who I am. Everywhere I look the signs are warning, 'Danger, turn around'.

May 10

I can't believe my luck—my alcohol-free fortnight has coincided with the NRL (National Rugby League) test. I know that alone should not affect my enjoyment of the game, but I can't help but feel there is something fundamentally wrong with the concept of me watching footy without beer. I can't quite put my finger on it but celebrating a try, with lemonade, well ... it just seems wrong. It would be like watching the Super Bowl without a giant hotdog or soccer without a pint. Some things in this world are just meant to go together, and one of them is beer and sports.

Come on, Aunt Flo. If you drop by for a visit, I promise to take you out for cocktails.

May 15

For the past sixteen days, my temperatures have been floating in the high ranges of normal, and with no sign of Aunt Flo, I am starting to experience feelings ranging from excitement to trepidation. I have read enough data to know what these results could mean. But, of course, it could be nothing. Honestly, the chances of falling pregnant on the first try are so minute; I don't know why I am so worried.

May 16

Pencilling another temperature of thirty-seven point eight degrees on my chart, I realise a home pregnancy test (HPT) may be in order. I don't expect a positive result but before leaving the house I throw a test kit in my handbag anyway. Don't ask me why, but I am convinced the chance of a positive result will be dramatically reduced if the test is taken at work.

Well, here I am. It is Friday morning, and I am not sure how I feel. Science tells me I could be pregnant, but my head tells me that it isn't possible. Shaking off my nerves, I grab the box of Clearblue early detection tests and, once again, sneak off to the bathroom. Stepping into the corridor, I look over my shoulder guiltily. My heart is racing, and I am flushed. It feels like everyone knows my secret.

Stepping into the last cubicle, the one with its own sink, I quickly close the door behind me, and rip open the instructions. After following steps one to three, I check my watch. *Okay, I just have to wait until ten past eleven. Easy.* Checking the door is locked I start pacing. Each passing second reverberates through me like the chime of an old town clock. I am edgy and impatient but force myself to wait.

Rubbing my eyes passes a few more moments. And after taking a deep breath, I look nervously at my watch, then at my reflection in the mirror. The towering trees through the open window command my attention for a few moments, then the graffiti on the back of the door. I search for anything to stop myself from looking at the sink and the life-changing stick waiting upon it.

Two of the world's longest minutes pass, and my eyes creep back towards the stick. *Is there any colour there?* I force my eyes away. I have to wait. My heart beats faster. My head spins. I sit down. Blood is pounding in my cheeks. I am hot and giddy with anticipation. Seeking a distraction, I look to the world outside the window. It seems different, like a scene from a turn-of-the-century movie.

An eternity passes. I look down at my wrist. My heart skips a beat. The time is up. Finally, I will know! I am not sure why I am so scared, but it feels like I'm trapped in a dream. My head screams at me, *this could be real*! My heart pounds. As I turn towards the sink, I wonder if I actually want to know what's there. Once I look, I know that my life may change forever. But if I keep sitting where I am, it gets to stay the same.

Come on girl, pull yourself together.

Feigning confidence, I stand, and let two very wobbly legs lead me to the basin. Taking a deep breath, I look down. *OMG! Two lines! #$%&! Two lines!* I place a hand on the sink. *OMG! That means positive doesn't it?* Panicking, I look around. *Where are those instructions? OMG! What is happening?*

Sitting back on the toilet seat, I put my head between my knees. My heart is palpitating like I have just spent an hour in a sauna. I feel sick. I can't concentrate. I'm numb. I don't know what to think. *OMG! Pregnant!* I feel myself separating from my body and wish I could lie down. *#$%&! What am I going to do?*

For a while, I sit quietly as my world fractures. But then somewhere in the fog, a thought takes shape. *Oh God! I'm at work. People will be looking for me.* Sitting up, I try to pull myself together but it feels like I might never walk again.

All I can think is, *first try—is this possible?* I am totally freaking out, and I can't tell anyone. *OMG!* After what seems like an aeon, I am back at my desk.

The rest of the day is a blur. My office shrinks in and out and I am unable to concentrate on anything. I get nothing done. I feel like I am outside of my body, trapped in some kind of liquidised bubble. I feel like an extra in a Jim Morrison film clip. I can't believe that instead of chickening out, I am now pregnant. Me! The girl who not that long ago wasn't having kids. It just doesn't seem possible.

With my mind spinning in circles, the afternoon is one of the longest and strangest of my life.

Later that day

I know I should tell Brad the news the moment he gets home, after all it is the right thing to do, but I just can't bring myself to do it. I need some time to digest everything.

Sitting alone, at the dining room table, shadows form as the sun descends into its nightly slumber. Unable to fathom the day's events, I open my bag for the hundredth time and look at the secret hidden within. Even though the two dark stripes are indisputable, I am still unconvinced as to their authenticity. And if they aren't real, then I don't have to tell anyone, right?

Anyway, Brad's parents are arriving tonight, which means a distinct lack of privacy and the perfect excuse to keep my little secret, just that, for a while longer.

May 17

It's Saturday. A Saturday like most others, except this one, is different. This Saturday I have a bun in the oven.

Brushing my teeth, I look into the bathroom mirror, a mirror I have looked into a thousand times before. Moving from side to side I try to decide whether or not I look pregnant. *Pregnant! How on earth can I be pregnant?* I cannot get my head around it.

10.00 am

"No Kenmore By-Pass!"

I smile, as my niece waves her homemade protest sign in the air. The sun is shining off her golden locks, she has a determined look on her face and she looks beautiful.

"Aunty Immi," she says, looking up at me with her enormous baby blues, "what will happen to the koalas if they put a yucky road here?"

"Well," I start, "they will get moved to another park."

Not liking my answer, she immediately pouts.

Got to fix this, and quickly. "But we're not going to let that happen are we?"

"No way!" she shouts triumphantly.

"Now come on, let's go and have a play."

"Yeah!" she squeals in delight, instantly forgetting about the plight of our furry little friends. "Can we jump off the fort like last week?"

Aarrghh ... no ... because, I will probably throw up all over you... "Sure darling, but let's ask Mum and Dad first."

During the trip home, I almost spill my secret. The nausea is so unbearable it takes every fibre of my being, not to scream at my father-in-law, *pull over!* But I can't, not here. There would be too many questions. I just have to push through it. I close my eyes, squeeze the door handle, and pray that my house would move five kilometres closer.

As I lean against the back seat window, all I can think about are those two pink lines. I know I am experiencing "morning sickness", but still can't believe I am pregnant. When I think about what lies ahead for us both, I am as frightened as I am excited. But emotionally, when it comes to the baby, I don't seem to have any real feelings: not happiness, not sadness, not even shock. Just a distant, strange feeling, like I have received a hard knock to the head. I wonder how other women react to the news.

May 18

Although I am feeling guilty about not telling Brad about his impending fatherhood, the last couple of days have allowed me some time to reflect and get used to the idea. Not to mention the opportunity to do four more pregnancy tests. Just in case!

May 19

I feel strange today ... offbeat. I am not sure if it is due to the fact that I am pregnant or because no one knows about the baby but me. Either way, arriving home makes me feel happier.

Hoping to find something to calm my queasiness I open the kitchen cupboard. I have just pulled out the medicine box when I hear Brad at the door.

"Hey darl how was your day?"

"Not too bad," I reply, shoving the box back in the cupboard. "How about you?"

"Yeah, okay," he says, hanging his keys. "Just a typical Monday ... nothing out of the ordinary."

Well not yet.

We banter for a few minutes before our usual routine takes over; Brad turns on the TV and grabs a drink, whilst I get leftovers out the freezer. I busy myself for a while, but once Brad perches himself on the edge of the dining room table, with a glass of freshly squeezed orange juice; I know it is time to make my move. Reaching into my handbag, I am sure my thumping heart will give me away, but when I look up the daddy-to-be is lost to the day's headlines, completely unaware that anything unusual is on the horizon.

My hand trembles as I search for the little life-changing stick. For a second I think it lost, but then my fingers enclose around the familiar shape. Without saying a word, I place it in Brad's empty hand. He senses something, but for a moment keeps watching the news. My patience wanes. I am about to say something when he finally looks down. He quietly stares at it, and I can tell by the creases in his brow that he is not sure what he has or why. But then the light bulb moment arrives!

At first he doesn't say a word. But then his face alters, and he looks at me with the same look of shock and surprise that I sported just a few days ago. "Oh my God! Is this what I think it is?"

I stammer a barely audible yes.

Like a rocket, he is off the table, and I am off the ground. Laughter fills the room. We are going to be parents!

May 20

Holy #$%@. I'm pregnant!

May 21

Winter means a lot of different things to different people. But in our family it means only one thing: football. Along with a slight dip in temperature, the month of May brings us the oracle of all football matches, The State of Origin Series.

Some people find it odd that a household of girls grew up to be football mad, but to my family, it seems perfectly normal. To us there was nothing as normal as drinking beer and watching the game on a Sunday afternoon.

In Australia, particularly on the east coast, Origin is not only cause for a bit of acceptable state-to-state banter and sledging, but is also a great reason to celebrate. For most of us sun-loving Aussies, the lack of beach weather is no excuse not to get the barbeques fired up and put the beer on ice. On the east coast, anyone who is anyone has plans for State of Origin night.

But this year, I won't be joining the masses of footy fans as they dip their hands into eskies and look for a handy bottle opener, this year I will be toasting my post-try celebrations with green tea. And all I can say to that is: pregnancy sucks!

P.S. Go the Blues!

May 22

This has been a really weird week for us as the realisation starts to sink in that we—Brad and Imogen, the bourbon drinking, festival-going, first-to-arrive, last-to-leave party people—are going to be parents. We are jubilant and excited, but equally shocked.

Brad keeps asking, "How could it have happened so fast?" I am not sure if his questioning has to do with me getting pregnant first try or the fact that the "love festival" has been cut short. Either way, he is happily parading around like King Tut bragging about how impressive his boys are. I think he has forgotten that I was there too.

P.S. We (the Blues) won the first game of the Origin series. Yeah!

May 24

We are at our local medical centre, waiting for our doctor to confirm what we already know. I am flipping through my third trashy magazine, when I finally hear the words, "Come on through".

Taking a seat opposite the person we usually only see for a bout of the flu, we wait for her to begin.

"So what can I...?" she asks, opening my file.

"I think I am pregnant!" I blurt out before she can finish.

"What makes you think that?" she asks, her eyes twinkling.

"I feel really sick, and ..." I pause.

"Yes."

"And, I have taken five positive pregnancy tests!"

She almost laughs. "Ah yes, I think we can confidently say you are pregnant then."

Her words shock me. I am not exactly sure why. I knew I was expecting before I arrived. But somehow, hearing the words from her mouth makes the whole thing seem more real. Although overjoyed at the prospect of becoming a mum, I must confess that deep down there was still a part of me secretly hoping that my 99.9% accurate test kits might be wrong and that I might leave the clinic this morning with a "So, sorry, better luck next time".

But instead of avoiding my greatest fear, I leave the little doctor's surgery on Birkin Road with a specialist referral and undeniable proof that this is all very real indeed.

Climbing into the car, I can feel the blood pounding in my temples. My head aches. I fasten my seatbelt, and as Brad reverses out of the parking lot, I rub the side of my head. I am so tired.

When I notice we are turning left instead of right, I look towards Brad.

"Oh, thought we should pull into the bottle shop quickly?" he says.

I reply with an inquisitive look.

"Well." He grins mischievously. "We have to celebrate, the good news."

"But we've known for days."

"Yes," he agrees. "But now we know for sure."

Unable to begrudge him for being excited, I simply shake my head.

Three minutes later we walk through familiar doors. I am not surprised in the least when the staff welcome us with warm smiles.

"Hi guys," Joel says looking up from his order sheet. "Big plans for the weekend?"

"Not really," I reply. "Just hanging around."

"Michelle has some fantastic new reds from the Barossa if you want to treat yourselves."

Seeing a twenty-something-year-old brunette standing to the side of the front counter, Brad wanders over. Noticing I haven't moved, the boys look my way. "You sick or something?" they ask in unison.

"Yeah, just a touch of the flu," I reply, trying to sound normal.

"That's a shame."

"Yeah ... it's just one of those things." I smile back.

I may be smiling on the outside but inside I am simmering. Sure, I am excited about our news but I can't help but feel miffed about not toasting my own pregnancy! Walking back to the car, I decide that I dislike being pregnant.

May 26

Book the hospital.

Find an obstetrician.

Source child care.

Organise antenatal classes.

Looking down at the list in front of me, I shake my head. *So much to do, it's no wonder mums are always so tired.* Realising that procrastinating will get me nowhere; I pick up my tea in one hand and the phone in the other and make my first call.

"Sorry, we are booked solid in January."

Crossing my number one choice off the list, I grimace. I am extremely disappointed. Dr Cook has the best reputation in town and has been recommended to me by everyone from the local baker to the hairdresser. Unfortunately, the next call doesn't fare much better. "Sorry, all of our doctors are absent in January." Squelching emerging panic, I cross two more names off the list.

I want to give up but have no choice but to continue. When another smug receptionist tells me baby making is an extremely busy business, and January isn't an ideal time to give birth, I almost lose it. I want to shout, "Do you think I planned to give birth in the New Year just to disturb your holiday plans?" But instead the scene only plays out in my head, and I hang up with a polite but disappointed, "Thanks anyway."

Fantasising about a roadside birth, I almost miss the first positive news of the day, "Yes, Ms Barnacle, we have a place for January."

May 27

I wake up gagging.

Brad turns off the alarm and looks my way. "Are you okay?"

"Not really, I am ridiculously nauseous."

"Well, that's what you get for sneaking out to drink wine and dance on table tops," he teases.

"Amusing!" I reply, unaltered by his attempt to make me laugh.

"Well, it wouldn't have been too far-fetched six months ago," he smirks.

Resisting the urge to throw my pillow at his head, I instead pull it around my ears, in an attempt to stop the room from spinning.

May 28

"Hey babe, only two days until your birthday," Brad chirps, as he looks up from the diary I keep on the kitchen bench. "What do you want to do?"

"I don't know," I reply. "But I suppose I will have to cancel O'Malley's."

"Yeah, I guess you're right," he agrees. "It's a shame though; I know how much you love that place."

"It is the best Irish pub in town." I frown. "I just hope everyone accepts my 'I have the flu' spiel."

"They will," he grins. "But they'll just be a little confused. It's certainly out of character to let something get between you and a birthday beer."

Cancelling my party comes as a wake-up call. It has made me realise that the sacrifices and loss of freedom have already started. Sure, being pregnant doesn't mean I'm dead, but there will certainly be no dancing until dawn, no stomach-racing down water slides or cantering on horseback for me. For me, life has become more like a box of wholegrain crackers than of chocolates.

May 29

My sister Tori and her husband Dean are coming up for the weekend. I am the happiest I have felt in weeks! I always love catching up with my family. Usually our get-togethers focus around gossiping and drinking way too much wine, then whinging about the consequences all the next day. But this birthday will be a little different. This year our post-celebrations won't involve fry-ups and paracetamol.

Luckily, my little sister is aware of our situation—that is, she knows we were planning for a baby but not that I am actually pregnant—so I don't have to come up with a lame excuse as to why there's no champagne. Though keeping the truth from her is not going to be easy because telling a sister good news is always so much fun!

May 30

Thirty-six and pregnant! What a way to start a birthday.

With bubbles off the agenda, we head to the cinemas to catch the latest Indiana Jones movie in Gold Class.

"What can I get you?" the waitress asks.

"A mugaccino and a slice of mud cake, please," I reply.

Feeling guilty, I give my tummy a rub. Sorry, little one, I know I should be drinking decaf, but everyone knows you're allowed one naughty thing on your birthday. Pausing, I rephrase. But, of course, this will not apply to you until you are at least thirty-two.

8.30 pm

With dinner behind us, we decide to relax with a DVD. Yes, another movie. That's life without wine. Thinking a shower might help me through two hours in the dark, I head towards my room. On my way past the lounge room, I notice my sister is already settled on the couch. Cushions, wine, potato chips! She is ready to rock.

She calls out, "Hey, where are you going?"

"Up for a quick shower," I reply, hoping for a quick getaway.

"Don't worry about a shower now, sis. Have one tomorrow."

"I really need one," I said. "I need to wake up."

"Why are you so tired?" she asks. "We've been bludging all day."

Opening my mouth, I scramble for a deflection. But before I get the chance to speak, Brad, the world's worst secret keeper, says, "Because she's six weeks pregnant, that's why!"

Tori's reaction is immediate and reminds me of a scene from an old Looney Tunes cartoon. With eyes bulging, and lungs screaming, I half expect her head to explode. Watching her jump up and down it is hard not to get caught up in the moment.

"Hey, I know this is exciting." I chuckle at her rejoicing. "But you are the only one who knows, and it has to stay a secret for a while longer."

"Sure." She grins back.

I raise my eyebrows, unconvinced. But her excitement is contagious and before I know it I am laughing as she dances around the room, singing, "I'm going to be an aunty. I'm going to be an aunty."

June 1

Okay, I know I am pregnant. I have the symptoms. I have seen the doctor. But to be completely honest, it does not feel real. *Me? Pregnant!* I just can't seem to get my head around it.

June 3

When I was sixteen, my best friend Karen and I drank tequila for the first time. I remember the evening well, it had been pitch black, and Scott the cute dark haired boy from next door had lured us over the fence with the promise of a surprise. The evening was hot and humid and dressed in singlets, and cut-off denim shorts, we had spent the night lying on his trampoline starting at the sky and giggling at Karen and her delightful Scottish accent.

The memory of that evening would stay with me always, just like the vow I took never to touch that particular white spirit ever again. And waking up this morning, I remember exactly why it was a promise I had always kept. There was no way I was going to work, as work and feeling hideously, horribly ill, just don't mix.

1.00 pm

I spend the morning slipping in and out of semi-consciousness. But eventually, hunger, brings me back to the land of living. I like the idea of food, but the urge to eat isn't strong enough to coax me out of bed. Still feeling groggy I switch on the TV in search of a movie. When greeted with an enormous set of teeth and the latest 'must have' blender, I begin to zone out.

Time ticks by as I stare blankly at the screen, but then, a loud, insistent grumble refocuses my attention. *Okay. Message received.* Standing tentatively, I challenge my feet to take my weight. I manage two steps from the security of the bed before all thoughts of lunch disappear. Teetering on collapse I stumble backwards.

2.00 pm

After washing my face with cold water, I look into the mirror. My eyes are sunken, and I look like an extra from *The Walking Dead*. Wiping my hands on a towel, I ignore the hot burn in my throat and let my thoughts drift back to lunch. *Maybe some soup would be good.* Feeling hopeful I attempt a few unsteady steps. Unfortunately, I don't make it far before I realise I have shown my hand prematurely, and only an experienced gambler should bet against the house.

Sitting on the cold tiles, with my head between my bare knees, hot tears roll down my cheeks. I can't do it ... I just can't. I weep. How can I hold down a job and run a house like this? I'm just too sick. I can't do it. I just can't.

Tears turn to sobs as the reality of my situation slams home. Sad and alone, I curl up on my new designer faux mat.

I don't know who penned the term morning sickness, but it is far beyond misleading! I go to bed sick, wake up sick, and spend most of the time in between with my head down the toilet.

June 4

After yesterday, I decide that my boss should know what is going on. So after dropping some mail in the tray marked 'outgoing', I head for her office. As I pass the main reception desk, my heart is pounding. *I can't believe I am going to share my secret.*

Stopping at her door, I take a deep breath. "Hey, Jenny, you got a minute?"

"Sure, come in."

After asking if it is okay to shut the door, I close it behind me and take a seat in the visitor's chair. I can tell by the look on her face, she is wondering what is going on. I have been practising my speech all morning, but before the first word rolls off my tongue, she laughs and says, "You're not pregnant, are you?"

"Well, yes, actually," I reply in total shock. How on earth could she know? Is it that obvious?

"Wow! Really? You are? I was only joking." She laughs. "But that is fantastic! I am so happy for you."

Filling my lungs with fresh air, my shoulders begin to relax.

"Wow," she says. "You are going to be a mum."

I almost say no. Yes, I am pregnant, but that doesn't mean I am going to be someone's mother. But then I realise that it actually *does.*

June 6

I have decided, without a doubt in my mind, that I utterly HATE being pregnant! I am sick of being sick, tired of being tired, and bored with my boring, non-existent life. I want control of my body back. I have had enough! I want access to the rewind button!

Honestly, if I had known this was how it was going to be, I never would have allowed myself to get pregnant in the first place. Of course, I don't want anything to happen to my innocent unborn child, but I am infuriated, sad, and depressed.

I can't believe my mother did this four times. And by choice!

Placing my hand on my belly, I deliver an ominous message. Baby, listen here! You are absolutely never, I mean ever, getting any brothers or sisters! Period!

To anyone who is seriously considering having a baby, I sincerely and passionately *do not* recommend it. Whatever you do, do not do it! And I mean EVER! And if you don't heed my advice, then don't say I didn't warn you.

June 9

After spending half an hour chatting to my pharmacist, I walk out of my local chemist with high hopes and a significant dent in my credit card. Always one to go green where I can, I went for the natural and chemical-free remedies, he recommended. But to be honest, if he had suggested washing my hair in elephant poop; I would be expecting a shipment from Africa any day.

June 10

"Oh, come on, babe," Brad moans again. "Can't we just tell the immediate family?"

After weeks of trying to keep Super-excited Pants quiet, I am finally swayed by his latest plea, and within moments, the phone is glued to his ear.

"Hey, babe, you getting off that phone soon?" I tease. "I am sure you've told everyone but the video store guy, by now."

"Well, I am sure Sean will be excited for us."

"Oh, yes, very amusing!" I laugh playfully, "Now, hand it over."

My first call is to my mother. As expected she matches Brad's family in the excitement stakes. "Oh my God, honey, that's wonderful. I absolutely can't wait to be a grandmother again."

Hanging up the phone, I try to bury the emerging sarcasm. Yes, of course, you are all happy; you aren't the ones about to throw up in your teacake!

Wallowing in self-pity, I press on with another call.

"Hi, Abbey, it's me."

"Hey, sis. How are you?"

"Yeah ... not too bad," I say. "I've got some news."

"You won lotto?" She laughs.

"I wish."

"So what is it?"

"You are going to be an aunty."

"Oh, sis, this is awesome!" she squeals. "I have only been waiting fifteen years. Oh, how exciting!" Her enthusiasm is intoxicating, so I let her continue.

"So what are you going to call it? Oh, I think I still have some of Jaiden's old toys. Far out, I've got to book a flight so I can see your belly. Wow. I'm going to be an aunty. Woo, hoo!"

June 11

"So, you ready for the big game tonight?"

I look up from my desk to catch John hanging a Maroon's banner (the enemy) in my window.

"Well, we won the first game of the Origin series, so let's just see," I say. "And hey, get that @#$% off my window."

Laughing, John walks away. As I watch his signature blue jeans and plaid shirt disappear up the hall, I smile. He always has a marvellous knack of cheering me up.

June 13

The sound of the alarm pulls me away from a very nice place. I open my eyes, before shutting them immediately. The pain in my head is profound. The room is too bright. I feel like I am caught in the spotlight of a police helicopter. Feeling movement beside me, I will the noise to stop. *Hurry up and hit the snooze button!*

"Thank God it's Friday," Brad mutters as he sends the room back into silence.

"Yeah, great," I reply sarcastically.

Pulling a pillow over my head, I banish thoughts of making the express bus and join him for another nine minutes of bliss.

11.00 am

What's the time? Oh ... only half an hour since morning-tea... Shaking my head, I turn back to my computer.

11.06 am

That's it. I can't stand it! The monster living inside me is awake and ravenous. Wanting to appease it quickly, I open my desk drawer and start rummaging.

There's got to be something in here. But I have to concede that is more wishful thinking than known fact.

Pushing aside a box of pens, I spot a muesli bar. *Awesome!* Smiling like a six-year-old under a broken piñata, I begin ripping open the wrapper. Taking a bite, it never occurs to me to check the expiry date. The sugar hits my veins, rapidly, thus immediately silencing the whimpering from within. For a split second, I am satisfied. But then the little voice in my head takes over. Y*ou're going to get fat...* it mocks. Defiantly ignoring its taunts, I take another bite.

June 14

My eyes open, it is morning. The light in the room tells me the sun has been up for a while. Rolling over, I look at the clock radio that has been telling me the time, since I was a teenager. Its familiar red glow informs me that it is almost eight. Smiling, I shut my eyes. I love weekends!

Draining the last of his coffee, Brad closes the paper.

"Think I might mow the lawn. What are your plans for the morning?"

"Actually," I reply, feeling quite perky. "I was thinking of trying one of those prenatal DVDs I bought."

"Great idea. I know you've wanted to do something normal for a while now."

Agreeing with his response, I make my way up the hallway with a cheerful gait, though my merriment is a little surprising.

Pre-pregnancy, my motto was enduringly steadfast: "the words *fun* and *run* should never be used in the same sentence." In fact, I can quite confidently say that I hate exercise with a passion. The only reason I drag myself through a few sweaty sessions on a semi-regular basis is to balance out my wine and chocolate consumption. But ever since the ability to don my Lycra and go to the gym was taken from me, surprisingly, I have missed it.

June 15

Pulling out a chair, I place my mug on the dining table.

"Hello, stranger." Brad smiles. "I haven't seen you at breakfast for a while."

"Yeah!" I beam back. *Two days in a row, this almost counts as a miracle.* "Do you want one?" I ask, pointing to my cup.

"Sure, but I'll get it."

Handing me the paper, he heads to the kitchen.

"So who do you think the baby is going to look like?" he asks, filling the kettle with fresh water.

"No idea," I confess. "But if it gets your legs and my lips, that will be a good start."

His laughter suggests he agrees.

Turning back to the headlines, I pick up my tea. As the warmth from the liquid seeps into my body, I start to feel better. More connected. Before now I had never realised just how lonely pregnancy can be. It is quite funny to think that it takes a fair amount of intimacy between two people to make a baby but once a child is conceived, the same two individuals can become like total strangers, both travelling on what often feels like solo journeys towards parenthood.

June 17

The good times are over. I wake up, not to the view of the sun shining through my beautiful timber blinds but to the cold harsh reality that I am back in bed twelve, ward six, aka Maternity Hell!

Seeing my eyes open, the warden's head whips my way.

"Please, sir," I beg. "Please, let me go home."

Shaking his head unsympathetically, he points towards the old grey clock on the wall.

"But, please sir," I whisper. "It's just not fair..." But any pleas for clemency fall on deaf ears.

Acknowledging defeat and too weak to protest further, I sink into a pile of pillows and drift away.

June 18

My bedroom floor is covered in clothes: Skirts that will never be worn. Work pants that don't fit. Maternity jeans that hang around my knees. The mess makes me want to cry.

Eager for moral support, I place my hand on my new and now prominent bump. Do you have any idea, little one, how horrible it is for a woman to have nothing to wear?

To be fair, I wait a full ten seconds, for an answer. But as usual, I get no response.

As a teenager, I loved clothes. I dreamt of a career in fashion. But as an adult, clothes have become my Achilles heel. If I could have a dollar for every time I have come home from the mall, empty handed—feeling fat, short, and misshapen—I could probably afford my own designer. However, despite the heartache, and frustration these days have caused. They have taught me one valuable lesson. Kicking the pile of "evil" clothes at my feet, I grab a pair of yoga pants, throw on a baby-doll dress and head out the door.

There! Fat and weird looking, but no one will ever know!

June 19

I came very close to slipping up at work today.

For a change, John, aka JB and I were talking music. John is the coolest guy, and lucky enough to have spent the seventies watching all the fantastic bands whose music filled my house as a child. I totally love that he remembers the name of every Led Zeppelin album and never gets tired of bragging about how awesome Black Sabbath were at the old Festival Hall in Brisbane. He absolutely lives and breathes music.

He is also addicted to owning music the way many women are addicted to shoes. Although unlike our weakness for "two for one" offers at Nine West, John's purchases are almost always an "accident", often encouraged by red wine and eBay.

I always know JB has had one of his "accidents" when half a dozen CDs arrive in the office mailbag. It has become a bit of an ongoing joke between us, and I always laugh when I picture him sneaking his latest "bargain" past his wife Sue.

When it comes to music, we never run out of conversation material, and today our discussion revolved around the upcoming Def Leppard concert.

"So, Im, are you and Brad getting tickets?"

I was so excited at the prospect of seeing the boys again that I almost said, "I'm not sure as I'll be seven months pregnant by then."

But by some miracle, two students walked into the mailroom at that exact moment, and I somehow managed to hold my tongue and mumble, "Do you know who's supporting them?"

June 23

Today all I did was eat breakfast, change the sheets, and answer an email before needing a nap.

June 24

I hate waiting. I hate being scared! I hate not knowing if things are going to be okay. My first ultrasound is on Thursday but that seems FOREVER away. I guess I shouldn't worry, I should trust that things will be fine. But it's easier said than done. I just want to cry. No one ever told me how scared you feel as an expectant mother. Oh, week thirteen, where are you?

June 26

Today is my first obstetrician appointment. I have spent the whole morning freaking myself out. My mind has been filled with images of all sorts of nasty medical procedures. I can't wait until it is over and done with, and I am home safe and sound.

Entering the doctor's reception room, I take a seat by the window. Sitting in a room full of women chatting about baby stuff, I feel weird and out of place, though I do find some comfort in being surrounded by people who can sympathise with the way I am feeling. Grabbing a cup of water from the fountain, I smile at the receptionist as if I belong.

Fortunately, I only have to busy myself for a few minutes before I hear my name being called. Eager to be out of there, I follow the doctor into her office and take a seat. Looking around her room, I am surprised by the sparse décor. But before I can dwell too long on the lack of baby photos, my thoughts are interrupted by the first of her questions.

"Do you have any heart problems or other issues that you know of?"

"No."

"Is there a history of diabetes in your family?"

As the questions continue, I begin to relax. *This isn't too bad at all.*

Soon the questions are over, and she is telling me it is time for the ultrasound.

Oh, this is exciting, I think happily, standing up. But then she continues, "And a quick Pap smear and internal exam."

Instantly my excitement fades, and my heart rate doubles.

Reluctantly I follow her into the next room. Climbing onto the exam table, I am both nervous and excited.

Without hesitation, she reaches over to turn on the ultrasound machine. I look at Brad who is smiling. *This is it.* We keep watching the monitor but nothing seems to be happening. *Is this normal?*

"Oh, bugger," the doctor says with a frown, in response to my silent question. "It's not working. We'll just have to move onto your internal."

Disappointed, I lie down, close my eyes, and think pleasant thoughts.

June 27

I am entering mid-semester exam results into the computer system when the office phone rings. It's the obstetrician's office.

"Good news, Imogen. The machine is fixed and we can get fit you in this afternoon."

Hanging up the phone, I call Brad immediately.

"Are you excited?" Brad asks, handing me a magazine.

We are back in the doctor's waiting room, but this time with joyful anticipation.

"Absolutely! But I keep worrying the doctor is going to tell me it is all a big mistake."

Brad squeezes my hand. "Don't be silly. It will be okay."

I smile back nervously before a shadow falls over me. I look up to see Dr Whelan standing in front of us. "Come on through."

Grabbing my bag, I follow her into to the exam room. As she busies herself with gloves, I climb onto the table.

"Since the baby is so small, we will need to do a transvaginal scan."

Oh great, I think sarcastically. *My poor lady bits*! But within moments, all negative thoughts are forgotten as the image of our baby appears on the screen.

It is impossible to describe how wondrous it is seeing your baby for the first time. I have often heard that people are brought to tears by the sheer beauty of it. And now I totally understand why. We watch the little bean shape in front of us, in silence, and in awe.

Ba-Boom! Ba-Boom! Ba-Boom!

As our child's little heart thuds, tears well in my eyes, and Brad is left speechless for the first time in his life.

June 30

I am utterly confused as to why women are portrayed as being so happy during pregnancy because the only glow I am experiencing, is the glow of the bathroom light at three o'clock each morning.

July 2

I wake up nauseated, tired, and anxious. I can't stop thinking about the fact that I am going to be responsible for a real, live baby. Me, a girl who owns thigh-high boots! Me, a girl whose stilettos have been drunk out of by rock stars! Me, a girl who thinks getting up at ten o'clock on a Saturday is early.

July 4

I know I shouldn't complain, and I know this is such a small chunk of time out of my life, but I am just so sick of being sick! I literally can't remember what it feels like to be well. I want to stomp my feet and scream at the universe, "It's not fair!" I desperately want to feel healthy again. I want the rights to my body back. I want to have a life!

I know I have said it before, but I am going to say it again. After all, it's my diary and I should be able to cry if I want to. Had I known how awful this was going to get, or how slowly time would pass, I honestly would have thought much longer and harder about having a baby. Sure, I have a little life inside me that I already love and would give my life for but I just hate what is happening to my body because of it. I just wish I could be one of those women who cruise through their first trimester.

July 6

A new day and a new pregnancy symptom! Today it feels like I have been hooked up to a high-voltage fidget machine. No matter how much I try, I just can't seem to sit still. And this strange phenomenon appears to be affecting my brain too. I feel like a five-year-old on Christmas Eve.

July 9

Today is our twelve-week Nuchal scan. The scan is essentially an ultrasound which checks for abnormalities in the foetus. I know it is only a routine exam but I can't believe how scared I am. I spent so much time deliberating about whether or not I wanted this baby; I can't imagine facing the agony of deciding what to do if we receive a less than positive test result. I used to believe that I wouldn't knowingly bring a child with serious health problems into this world but this was before I had felt a life growing inside me. Now I can't even imagine having to make such a soul-destroying decision. I can only pray that everything will be okay.

Taking a sip of water, I glance at the clock on the reception desk.

"I hope he hurries up," I whisper. "My bladder is about to explode."

"You know doctors," Brad replies. "They are always running late."

"Yeah, and that would be okay any other time but now."

Taking a breath, I ready myself for a fresh round of whining but am un-expectantly interrupted by the sight of a middle-aged man looking my way. *Finally!*

Pushing a few stray grey hairs from his forehead, the man dressed in a blue plaid shirt, and snug fitting trousers gestures towards an open door. "Come on through."

My heart is hammering in my chest, as I follow his bulky frame into a surprisingly spacious room. Once inside, he points towards a low lying table on the back wall. Taking the lead, I slip off my shoes and climb on. Looking around at all the equipment, I can't help but feel a little anxious. I feel like I am about to be interrogated, but, as soon as the LCD screen above me lights up, my fears are dispelled.

Now things are getting interesting.

Lifting my shirt, the doctor applies the gel. It is cold but super effective—the scanning instrument slides over my belly as effort-lessly as a hand on a new baby's cheek. Seeing my baby again melts me to the core, and my persona begins to soften. Smiling I cock my head. *Mmm, I wonder what shape my baby will be today?* Watching the life-sized images of my little bean swirl in front of me, I quickly realise I have no idea what I am looking at. So, I look to the doctor for an inkling of what might be going on. He is in the zone. I attempt to read his face but it is clinical and blank. I am forced to wait.

Fifteen minutes later, the machine is off, and it is all over.

"Please, wait here," the doctor says, before pressing a button and disappearing into an adjoining office.

Hearing the printer groan to life in the next room, Brad reaches for my hand.

"How long has it been now?" I ask.

"I don't know. Ten minutes maybe."

"The wait is killing—" *Awesome, here he comes.*

Noticing the paperwork in his hands, my heart begins to race. I try desperately to see through his guise but once again there are no clues.

Hearing the report's first page being turned, I feel like I am watching time-lapse photography, as if all existence has slowed to nothing. I can hardly breathe. Whilst the doctor reads, the room is silent. I can hear the air-conditioning vent rattling above, and the sound of a heavy vehicle passing by outside. As the clock on the wall ticks loudly, forcing me to be patient, it feels as if my whole existence is pinned to his first words.

Hoping my scrutiny might provide an early answer, I watch him carefully. I am sure the intensity of my stare may cause his shirt to start smouldering at any moment but I continue to stare anyway.

Waiting is like ignoring an itch and I am just about to tell the man with the all the answers that I can't take it anymore when his body begins to relax.

"Nothing to worry about." He smiles easily. "All looks good. Your risk factor is equivalent to that of a nineteen-year-old. So, stop worrying and go home and grow that baby."

Not realising I haven't been breathing; I pull fresh oxygen into my lungs and grin. I want to hug him but instead offer my thanks and walk out the door.

July 20

It is the middle of winter. For some this may mean a day in front of the fireplace sipping on hot cocoa but here in balmy Brisbane, when the sun is shining, it doesn't matter what the calendar says, the outdoors are calling out to be explored.

To make the most of the beautiful winter day Brad suggests a trip into town. And after following his gaze past the elegant old magnolia to the cloudless view beyond, I quickly agree.

Walking through the botanical gardens, the sunlight warms our bodies and replenishes our souls. On our left the river sparkles between a splattering of boats, and from our right the sounds of playing children fill our ears.

"I guess that will be us soon." Brad smiles, reaching for my hand.

Watching the families so at ease with their reality, I can't help but wonder what parenthood will be like, and whether or not I will actually enjoy it. It is all I can think about these days.

For a while, all is quiet, and we continue walking, lost in our individual thoughts. I am still contemplating our future life as parents when Brad interrupts me with lunch plans.

"Hey darl, do you want to head to the Plough?"

Considering the Plough Inn is my absolute favourite pub, I am sure he already knows the answer, but I immediately respond with a confident yes.

"Hey, remember that Australia Day we spent there with Amanda and Troy?" he asks as we step onto the Goodwill Bridge.

It is a day I will never forget. The weather had been perfect. Not too hot, not too humid. I recall a beautiful breeze, which only complimented the cloudless summer sky. We spent the day surrounded by great friends and patriotic cheer. I will always remember the songs sung by an array of international bar staff keen to add to their patrons' joy. My memories included the Japanese students draped in Aussie flags, who danced on tables without spilling a drop of beer; the young autistic boy who wore a jester's hat and knew the words to every song the band played; and, of course, the pain I felt in my toes, as strangers whirled me around the dance floor, so joyous they were unaware they were stomping on my feet.

Memories have a funny way of eating up time. Before I know it, we have made the kilometre long walk through the Southbank parklands, ordered our meals, and are taking a seat on the two-hundred-year-old balcony. Looking down at the 'free' people below, drinking, smoking and laughing, my jealousy arrives fast and furious.

Not needing to fill every moment with useless chatter, we people watch as we wait for our meals, and it isn't long before we notice a roadie lugging equipment onto the small undercover stage below.

"I wonder who's playing today," I muse, looking around for a poster.

"Not sure," Brad replies. "I didn't check the board."

We start talking music, and when our meals arrive we are deep in conversation.

The scent of melted cheese and salt lights up my senses, and the moment it is placed before me, I begin devouring chunks of sauce drenched parmigiana. Brad, on the other hand, takes it a little slower, savouring every mouthful. With me being partially vegetarian, he rarely gets the opportunity to enjoy a good rump steak. For a while, we are lost to our appetites. But then the sound of an opening rift brings us back to the here and now. Looking down at the band below, Brad pushes his empty plate aside. "It sounds like they are about to start."

Unable to disguise my apathy, my shoulders slump.

"Want to grab some ice cream and cruise the markets?" Brad suggests quickly.

In an instant, I am on my feet. I don't realise it at the time but this small act has laid the foundations for my transition from beer and chips to cake and coffee.

July 24

Without a doubt, I am getting totally ripped off in the whole pregnancy department. A reprieve by week thirteen—that's what the brochure promised. But I am still sick and miserable! And whilst on the subject of false second-trimester promises, where is my glow? And what about all the other bump benefits, like radiant skin, shiny hair, and glossy nails?

They are nowhere to be seen! That's where.

When I look in the mirror, I don't see luminance. I see the face of a hormonal teenager. My golden summer locks have been replaced by some unrecognisable dark oily fuzz. My nose bleeds continuously. And I feel fat.

I don't feel any glow. I feel awful!

I want a refund. And, by the way, have I mentioned lately that I HATE being pregnant?

July 25

Today I had lunch with the girls at work. Our conversation began with Sian's new business venture, followed by Tracy's latest property purchase. After our coffees arrive, I decide it is time to add to the conversation.

"So guys, I have some news."

"What's happening Im?" asks Sian, taking a sip from her soy latte.

"Oh! Nothing much … I'm just having a baby."

"Phhhfff!" Coffee shoots from her nose. "Oh my God, that is so fantastic!"

"You rat!" Tracy laughs, handing Sian a napkin. "How could you keep this from us for so long? At least it explains why you have been looking like complete crap the past few months."

"Yeah, thanks." I grin back.

July 27

Food, food, food! I need more food. The watch Brad got me for my last birthday tells me I have been back from lunch only five minutes. But I'm ravenous. Opening my desk drawers, I begin

rifling. *There has got to be something in here somewhere. Score! Free promotional mints from Officeworks. Surely they're classed as a food group?*

Lately, my stomach has felt like a bottomless pit. It doesn't seem to matter how much I eat, I am literally STARVING all the time! I know my body is working 24/7 to create life, but at this rate I am going to be spending the next ten years pounding the pavement and licking lettuce leaves.

July 28

Ever since I was a little girl, I have loved reading. My mum read to me. My grandparents read to me, and my dad, who has the most incredible imagination, would sit on my bed for hours filling my head with stories of dragons, trolls, and the Land of Odd. To this day, I still smile when I think back to nights I spent hidden under my sheets with a torch in one hand, an Enid Blyton novel in the other, and the firm belief that Mum didn't know I was awake.

Even as an adult, I have almost stepped into traffic because I have had my head buried in a book. Whether it is a brochure at the doctor's office, the latest glossy magazine or a new Stephen King novel, reading has always been my friend, my escape. But, as of late, my thirst for the written word has done nothing more than frighten me.

Prior to becoming pregnant I had heard whispers about the woes of pregnancy and knew that childbirth was "supposed to hurt", but it was always something that happened to other people. But now as I troll the libraries, blogs, and parenting websites, I am becoming a little too aware of just how many things there are to cause me worry.

If it isn't enough that I am beside myself thinking about labour, my days are now filled with gruesome thoughts of giant needles, metallic forceps, and all sorts of other macabre instruments. I sometimes wish I could curb my curiosity. After all, I have heard about "that" cat!

Another discovery I have made since joining the ranks of the expecting is the existence of an age-old and secretive practice designed to ensure the continuation of the human race. Before having children I had only heard about the nausea and the back-ache, but now that it is too late to change my mind, mothers have stopped lying to me. Now, I am all of a sudden being made privy to all the truths and horror stories that previously had been 'conveniently' left unmentioned.

What is funny, though, is that despite any unpleasant experiences, every mother concludes her tale with the same six words: "But it is so worth it!" Well, I'll tell you something now, it better be! To make me forget about all the suffering and sacrifices, I have endured and will endure, it will have to be just AMAZING! And I mean Seven Wonders of the World kind of amazing!

August 4

Waking up, I get out of bed and walk across the room. I have almost reached the bedroom door when I realise something has changed. I look around. *That's it!* I grin. *The furniture is still all in the same place. Could this mean an end to my daily morning torment?* Feeling a new sense of jubilance, I am tempted to leap into the air. But, the knowledge that it may jar an already suffering lower back stops me.

August 6

This weekend marks one hundred days since ovulation. Yes, one hundred long days since, I have enjoyed a wine, jumped up and down, done a sit-up, swallowed a pill, or partaken in any of the other hundred wondrous things I used to take for granted.

Now, it's not that I jump up and down terribly often, but I do miss the freedom offered by an unrestricted lifestyle. I miss drinking caffeine without feeling guilty, ordering salad without checking it's been washed and taking medicine when I feel sick. I adore my little bambino but am just *so* over following all the rules.

August 7

Something exciting happened today. Tonight, whilst my home-made chilli-bean pizza warmed in the microwave, I felt my first kick. How cool is that! Well, actually it was just a few little flutters, but who cares about being precise? It was a milestone event and such a lovely surprise.

August 9

Now that I am expecting, I have suddenly become aware of another world, a world filled with children and pregnant women. They seem to be everywhere, just like chocolate on the first day of a new diet. I am not sure if we are in the midst of another baby boom or if they have always been there. But nevertheless, now that they are on my radar, they have become walking billboards for my personal research.

As I walk through my local shopping centre, I stare in fascination. Oh! Look at her hairdo. Her shoes! Oh! Is she really out here on her own with one of those tiny little creatures? The more I watch, the more I wonder. Can I become one of them? Will I magically morph from the total non-baby person I am now into one of these seemingly confident mothers? I just don't know...

August 12

Dressed like I am heading to a Bikram class, I smile at the irony—I can't even reach my toes, let alone attempt the downward facing dog.

August 13

Arriving at work colleague Deb's farewell, I eye off the delicious treats on the tearoom table. *Oh yum, a cheese platter, got to get me some of that.* Within seconds, I am pushing a knife through a slab of brie. But then, an irritating thought jumps into my head. Soft cheeses are on the no-go list. Putting down the knife I look around. *Oh, hang on, they have cheesecake. Perfect!*

Grabbing a slice, I head to the back of the room to take a seat by the window. I am happily savouring my second mouthful, when the moment is totally spoilt, by Jules, our senior accounts manager.

"Hey, Imogen, doesn't that have cream cheese in it?"

Jules has such an authoritative voice that I consider her words for just an instant. But the temptation to shove another piece of the mango flavoured delight into my mouth is too much so, shrugging my shoulders, I make a quick decision to accept an early membership to the Bad Mothers Club.

Rarely do we get the opportunity to socialise like this at work so the room is filled with the buzz of quiet chatter. Not in the mood to line up at the coffee machine, I stay seated. I am on my own for only a minute or two before the vacant chair beside me is filled. It is Mike, the latest addition to our marine biology department.

"So how's it all going, Imogen?" he asks, reaching for a slice of cheesecake.

"As well as can be expected." I smile, rubbing my belly. "How are you?"

"Great." He smiles cheerfully. "Would you believe my wife and I are expecting too?"

"Really! That's great. How far along is she?" *Oh no. Now I am doing it too.*

"About five months."

"Well, congratulations."

He thanks me for the well wishes, before going on to confess that he and his wife are still feeling pretty unsure about the whole thing. Hoping to relieve some of his doubts, I tell him, Brad and I are feeling the same.

"So what swayed you guys in the end?" I ask, placing my empty plate on the table.

"Well, basically, it was the 'will we regret it' argument that won in the end."

August 15

I have a new name for the baby—Summer. Not Summer after the beautiful warm season we enjoy over Christmas, but summer after a somersault.

Today whilst I tried to work, my little bean thought it would be an opportune time to practice its acrobatic skills. As my little bambino flipped and jumped and rolled, I felt like I was trapped in a rickety old boat heading into rough seas. Using every ounce of willpower I possessed, I pushed through the next three hours at my desk, but by the time three o'clock-itis hit, I'd had enough. *Little one. I am glad you are healthy and active. But please, for your mother's sanity, just stop.*

Ten minutes later, my pleas are answered.

About time! Now just relax and have your afternoon nap. Please.

As I go through my Inbox, opening my email, all is quiet. *Good baby.* I read four new messages and delete one. I am just about to reply to the sixth message when I feel a stirring in my belly. "That's it!" I shout, pushing the mouse across the table. "You win! I am going home early."

❀ ❀ ❀

After dozing for two hours, I still feel mentally exhausted but physically better. I head to the kitchen to make a start on dinner. I am chopping vegetables, half watching the news, and daydreaming, when it becomes apparent something is missing. *Mm, an end-of-the-week drink would be nice.* On instinct, I walk towards the fridge.

Oh, #$%&, what am I doing?

Deflated, I walk back to the bench, with all intentions of getting dinner in the oven before Brad gets home. I am just throwing some potatoes in a pot, when out of nowhere, I feel a strange sensation inside. It is pure, primitive, and raw. Blood rushes to my head. I feel hot and clammy. All I can think is, *I want a beer. Damn it! I have worked my butt off this week. I deserve it!*

Heart racing and hormones pumping, I am moments away from throwing the vegetable stacked chopping board across the room and screaming out loud.

Come on, Imogen. Calm down. It's just beer. Have a chocolate instead.

"I DON'T WANT A CHOCKIE!" I cry, dropping the knife. Any attempts to reason with myself are quickly lost, and before I know it the house is filled with the sound of my feet slapping against the tiles as I run to my room. Pushing the door open, I throw myself onto the bed, and with my face pressed against my favourite suede cushion, I cry an ocean.

Eventually, the weeping stops and I feel a moment of calmness. It seems like nothing awful can happen again for a very long time. I lie quite and still, like a predator stalking its prey. But then, before my soul can replenish, I feel something move. My little one is awake and ready to play. I want to howl, "Not again", but only manage a whimper. Within seconds, the empty room is once again filled with the sounds of sobbing, as I cry even louder than before.

August 16

I am in the nursery unpacking shopping bags, when I hear Brad's voice. I look up to see him in the doorway holding my favourite brown mug.

"What are you smiling about?" he asks, passing me the freshly brewed tea.

"Oh, I just remembered how much I used to love Winnie the Pooh, and it got me thinking about that girl you used to work with. You know the one we used to call Eeyore?"

"Yeah, how could I forget?" He laughs. "She really did love whining about the woes of a working mother."

"Well, she was probably justified," I add, now feeling remorseful for our youthful ignorance.

"Well, she'll get her revenge soon enough," Brad says, before reaching down to take the package from my hand.

"Hey, Immi, look at this."

Startled, I look up from my pile of random objects, to find the walls adorned with Hundred Acre Wood characters. Brad is standing still and squinting.

"Do you think it looks straight?" he asks, stepping over me, and closing one eye.

Now usually, I would just say, "Yes, that's fine", without even looking up. But today, I know the perfectionist in the family will literally get out his spirit level if he thinks the borders are crooked. So to save some time, I sweep away my usual apathy, and take a proper look.

"It looks perfect!" I reply truthfully, before peeking into the box on my lap.

Finding an adorable chocolate coloured bear, I call out to Brad. "Hey, darl, check this out—"

I look up to find him admiring his handiwork. He looks very pleased with himself. I begin to wonder why, and then notice the spirit level in his left hand. I can only shake my head. "God help me if I end up with two of you."

August 20

The past few days have been difficult. I haven't felt the baby move much and I can't get in to see the doctor until tomorrow. Not knowing what is happening is gut-wrenchingly frightening. Until now I hadn't realised just how much I am already in love with my child. We may be living in a modern age, but deep inside, every woman has a primal instinct to protect her offspring at all costs, and the fear I am feeling now seems ancient and raw.

August 22

Tomorrow we are off to the Gold Coast to meet up with my family. My sister Abbey and her husband are flying up from Sydney, so with Mum coming too, it will be the first time all the girls have been together for a while.

I am super excited though Brad is pretending to be worried, not because he doesn't have a good time with my sisters, but because last time we all got together our arms ended up looking like gap year passports. I have told him not to worry, that this trip will be different. Honestly, it's not like the Sin City bouncers are going to be ushering me inside, in my state.

August 23

"So where are we meeting them?" Brad asks, pulling up under a shady tree.

"Abbey's favourite. Pancakes on the Rocks."

"Isn't it called Pancakes in Paradise?"

"Yes," I reply. "But we did grow up in Sydney, you know."

"Okay," he snorts. "But what exactly does that have to do with it?"

"Well, we spent a lot of time gobbling down pancakes in a dimly lit café in the Rocks. So for us if it sells 'pancakes', it will always end in 'on the Rocks'."

Shaking his head, he locks the car and heads for the pedestrian crossing. "Sometimes, I wonder why I ask."

Entering the restaurant the first thing I notice is the smell of maple syrup, the second is that everyone has arrived. Seeing us approach, the girls stop chatting and Abbey screams, "Oh my God, you are here!"

Jumping from her chair, her hands are on my belly within seconds, "Hello, little baby, I'm your Aunty Abbey."

She gushes over me all the way back to the table. Once seated, we order more food than we need and spend the rest of the afternoon doing my two favourite things—gossiping with my best friends, and getting high on sugar.

That night

Wandering down the street, the aroma of garlic fills the air. *Cool, the restaurant choice is Italian. My favourite!*

Upon arrival, we are led to a table situated next to a giant concrete water feature. The place looks busy, which is always a good sign. The young waitress hands us a few menus before darting across the room to a large group of partygoers in the corner. As the girls secure their bag butlers over the red and white plastic tablecloths, I smile. *Not only Italian, but authentic Italian! Awesome!*

"Wow, the food here is phenomenal," I say reaching for a napkin.

"Absolutely!" Amanda agrees. "Though I don't know how we managed to fit it all in, after today's effort."

"The dessert sack, of course..."

Everyone laughs at Tori's comment. We have been joking about our family's legendary second stomachs for years.

"Talking about dessert," Dean interrupts, "how about we order some liquor coffees?"

"Half your luck," I mumble, reaching for the water jug.

"Hey," Amanda says, seeing my frown, "just think of all the calories you're saving."

I look her way and smile. "Oh, sis, you always have an uncanny way of looking on the bright side of things."

"That's me." She smiles, enjoying the compliment. "Now who wants to help finish off this red?"

August 25

I wake up, roll over, and peek at the bedside clock. *OMG! It's 7.45.* I jump up, ready to shout that we are going to be late for work, but then remember that it is Brad's birthday and we are taking the day off to celebrate. Instantly my heart rate slows, and the scream in my throat is stifled.

"You want first shower?" Brad offers, seeing that I am already standing.

"Sure, birthday boy," I reply, knowing too well his generosity is only because he wants a lie in. "You sleep a bit longer."

August 27

Being almost half way through my pregnancy, I had hoped to be at peace with my decision by now. But I feel like a fraud. To be completely honest, I am still experiencing frequent doubts about whether or not I have made the right decision, whether this is actually what I want. Sometimes I wonder if it is just because it all happened so fast, or simply because I am afraid of the unknown. It does concern me that I am not yet feeling a maternal bond with my baby. I know I should be happy, but all I can focus on is how hard it all is, and how long it will be before I get my body back.

When I think about the thousands of women undergoing IVF and all the couples left childless through no fault of their own, I do feel guilty. I know deep down that I should feel blessed, not depressed and full of doubt. But I can't help it.

Sometimes I wonder if my misgivings are due to the fact that I was never one hundred per cent sure of my decision in the first place. And at other times I think maybe it is because I am different from other women, that there might even be something wrong with me. I don't know how other mums-to-be feel. But I do want these feelings of confusion and uncertainty to go away. I desperately want them to be replaced with the same genuine convictions and joy I see in other women's faces. I want to wake up in the morning and feel excited!

August 28

I need this week to goes fast. I desperately want to be at week twenty. Week twenty will be such a significant milestone. It will mean I am at the top of the mountain. It will be like lunchtime on a Wednesday. It will be hump day. I will be at the summit ready to slide back down. I know it's still a week away, but I don't care. The countdown is on.

August 30

My social life is non-existent. And I feel old. I am so used to being the party girl that there is no other way of putting it. I feel like a boring old crone! Yes, the exact type of boring person I used to pity back when I was enthusiastically enjoying my twenties.

In no way do I feel like one of those cool glamorous yummy mummies portrayed on TV. No, in fact, I feel like a miserable old grandma! *Sorry, Nanna.* I just don't know how I am going to make it through another five months of this, especially as I only visualise life getting worse as I get bigger and fatter. *Pout!*

September 8

Today we are back at Medical Hill for my big scan. Medical Hill isn't the real name for this part of Brisbane. However, as the area is very hilly and all the offices lining the streets are filled with MDs it has slowly but steadily taken on the name.

We are on our third lap of the neighbourhood when a small red Hyundai pulls out in front of us. "Just there, darl on your left."

Applauding our luck, we park, feed the meter, and head towards the towering grey building adjacent to us. The nonchalant block of bricks is where we hope we will get the answer to "Big Nan's" question about whether she should knit pink booties or blue.

We sit back on the hard floral couch and it is not long before boredom sets in. I reach into my handbag and begin foraging. *Eew … my new lip gloss—perfect.* After smothering my mouth in cherry-vanilla I congratulate myself on my latest purchase, and glance up at the clock on the counter. The doctor is running late again. I return to my article and prepare to wait. But fortune seems to be on our side today and, after only a couple of paragraphs, I hear my name being called. Looking up from 'Hollywood's shock new bodies', I see a familiar face, signalling me over. *Wow, this guy sure loves his plaid.*

Knowing the drill, I bound through the door after him. So excited to be back on the exam table, it takes all my self-control not to grab the scanner, and start the exam myself.

I hear the sound of the machine being switched on, and as soon as the familiar black and white shapes begin appearing, I am instantly appeased. Watching the mass of swirling shapes move in front of my eyes, I can see all my baby's little features: fingers, toes, and the all-important heartbeat. It is nothing short of spectacular! As the doctor takes measurements and makes the occasional hum, I search for signs of the baby's gender, but to the untrained eye it is a fool's errand.

When the screen begins to fade, signalling the end of the imaging, I am filled with a pang of sadness. But this time the misery is short lived. This time the doctor may have news. Hoping my luck will continue, I turn in his direction. Brad and I must have looked like wolves after a long scarce winter because he delivers his report without hesitation.

"Well, the baby is perfectly healthy, is right on track with its measurements, and has presented itself well for sex determination."

He stops.

What is he waiting for?

I look towards Brad for an answer. But like me, he is sitting as mute and motionless as a bronze statue. I wonder why nothing is happening, and no one is talking, so I look back to the doctor for clarification. He has an amused look on his face but still says nothing. I want to break the silence, but feel like my mouth is filled with concrete. The man with all the answers watches us for a couple more seconds before raising his right eyebrow and taking a punt, "So do you want to know?"

Suddenly released from our collective trance, Brad and I look towards each other, smile and shout in unison, "Yes! Please, tell us."

I can almost hear the drum roll in my head. I am so excited. I can hardly wait two more seconds, let alone another twenty weeks! But then the torture is over, his lips are moving and my mind focuses: "You're having a girl."

Brad bounces out of his chair. His face is alight. I lie on the cold, white vinyl table grinning like a first-time Oscar winner. Whether it was Mother Nature, coincidence or a little bit of my gender intervention, at that moment, it doesn't matter—we are getting our little girl.

I cannot remember ever feeling so excited. The drive back to work is filled with jubilant chatter. I look at the photo the doctor has printed off for us at least a hundred times. It is so hard to believe. We are having a girl. A little girl to call our own! We are both so happy.

"Wish we could skip work and celebrate," Brad says, flicking on his indicator and veering into the university car park.

"Yeah, me too, but I suppose we need to be responsible now that we are going to be parents." I almost laugh at my own observation. Us, responsible parents? Hilarious!

Breezing into the office, a few minutes later, with a knowing smile and the news that we are keeping the gender a surprise, I am greeted with a wall of disappointment.

"We'll get it out of you." Nicole laughs.

"Oh! No, you won't." I grin back. "I'm a vault."

Five minutes later, my baby photo is balancing against my computer and I am pretending to check emails. I am deep in thought when the phone rings. It is Brad.

"Hey, darl, it's me."

"Hi. What's up?"

He hesitates, and then quickly confesses, "I ... err ... told my mum."

"What!" I sigh. "I thought we were supposed to be keeping it hush-hush."

"I'm sorry," he murmurs, though I swear I can actually hear him grinning through the phone. "I only made it five kilometres down the road, and I just had to tell someone."

Knowing that Brad is downright terrible with secrets, I choose to forgive him.

"Okay," I say, "but that's it, no one else."

He pauses.

"What ...?"

"Well, you know Mum, she's not good at secrets ... so I had to ring Dad."

He pauses again, and I exhale deeply waiting for the inevitable.

"Oh! And Craig too."

✸ ✸ ✸

Arriving home that night, I soon discover that Brad has been very busy between the time I last spoke to him and knock-off. It appears that his family haven't been the only ones made privy to our supposedly classified information. The proud dad-to-be has spent the afternoon telling just about anyone who would listen. I half expect to turn on the six o'clock news and see my name up in lights. I want to be cranky, but in hindsight I should have known. He was just too darned excited. Accepting defeat, I pick up the phone and get started on spreading the news myself. He is not the only one who is excited.

September 9

I am having a baby girl. A daughter! My own little princess! After so many months of feeling disconnected from the process, just knowing the sex of my child has made me feel more maternal. No longer is there some "it" sucking the life out of me; I can finally reach down, touch my belly and say *she* or *her*. It is such an incredible feeling, and at this point in the pregnancy, it has been the absolute best thing that could have happened. It is amazing that something as mundane as an ultrasound could have such a positive impact.

September 14

I have found a new interest in my pregnancy. For the first time in months, I actually feel excited about my little girl's arrival and spend the day sorting through boxes of donated baby clothes.

Cute but, unfortunately, still blue!

Thomas the Tank T-shirt—discard pile!

Gorgeous pink cardigan with matching dress and booties—the absolutely can't wait pile!

September 15

"Jasmine Crystal, get back here!"

"Isabelle Jade, stop that now."

As Brad hands me the yellow highlighter, I sigh. "Oh, I just can't decide."

For days, Brad and I have been trying to come up with a short list of names. For the past ten minutes, I have been yelling out our favourites to test how they will sound at the park.

Making a shortlist has been a lot of fun for both of us, but when it comes down to it, deciding on a name is hard. I mean, we will actually be naming someone; we will be bestowing upon our daughter something which will define her for the rest of her life. It is both an honour and a burden.

When I was growing up, different names were not common. I spent years having fun poked at me and swore that if I ever had the privilege of naming someone, I would take the matter very, very seriously. Call me unimaginative, but there will certainly be no Apples, Rainbows, or Tiger Lilies in my house.

September 18

Reaching for a sponge, I stop when I hear Brad enter the room. Sniffling I wipe a tear from my cheek.

"What's wrong?" he says, dropping his bag and racing towards me.

"I spilt the milk!"

September 20

There are prams, promises of ice cream and tired looking mums everywhere. The sun may have only been up a few hours, but the women here look exhausted already. It is the second week of the Target Baby Sale, and I am standing in the checkout line. Thinking I should have got a trolley, I readjust my purchases and take the opportunity to relax. I am daydreaming, and watching a little boy in front of me poke his little brother with a toy sword, when I hear a female voice behind me.

When are you due?"

I turn to see a dark-haired woman dressed in a white silk blouse and tailored trousers. Her hand is reaching out towards my belly, and she is smiling.

"January," I reply politely.

"Oh! You poor thing—carrying through the summer—I remember it all too well. Do you know what you are having?"

Using my most patient smile, I answer her question, "A girl."

"Oh, how lovely!" she says, taking a step backwards. "Have you picked any names yet?"

Looking at the ten deep queue in front of me, I take a deep breath. "Not yet, but we are getting close."

September 23

Clicking his favourite ballpoint pen, Brad circles the second name on our list.

"Are you sure? This is the one?"

"Absolutely."

"You know, we can always change our minds later on."

"No, I am sure. Paige Jasmine it is."

September 24

Stomach rumbling, I stare into the fridge.

Mmm ... Maybe some chocolate ... and if I hurry, it won't have any calories.

Reaching for the treat box, I jump, startled by a sound behind me.

"Hi, darl, I'm home."

I turn towards my long standing partner in crime and say hello.

"How are you?" Brad asks dropping his satchel on the bench.

"Good." But I would have been a lot better if you hadn't come home early. Now I am going to have to eat fruit.

"And little Paige, how is she?"

"Great!" I reply, reaching down to stroke my belly lovingly.

September 26

Brad's cousin Nick is getting married today, so we have the day off work. Usually, I look forward to big events like weddings because they are the epitome of drinking, dancing and overindulging. But since I will be abstaining from the more traditional parts of the festivities, I must admit I am miserable.

The ceremony was lovely. And the canapés I just refused, even nicer. As I wave past another tray of delicious imported beers, and champagne, it is hard not to feel like the odd one out. Watching everyone mingle and socialise on the deck, I can't help but feel nostalgic about my old life. As friends and family members reacquaint themselves, share stories, and call out for more wine, they hardly notice me. Me, being the boring fat sober woman in the back corner. As I sip ice-water and look out across the perfectly manicured golf green, I ask myself the same question I ask every day. *Is this all going to be worth it?*

The speeches drone on and on—the inevitable result of giving half-tanked relatives a microphone and an attentive audience. As long-lost pals continue to retell stories that no one else finds amusing but them, I wiggle and squirm in my seat. Paige has picked tonight of all nights to work her way under my ribs and practice her yoga moves.

As the night wears on, the empty seat beside me feels like a re-volving door. Being unable to make a quick exit, I am a prime target for tipsy party guests wanting a one-way conversation. As one grinning relative after another rubs my belly and slurs stories about their own crazy parenthood mishaps, I try to smile. But as the music shifts from top forty to Y.M.C.A and Nut Bush City Limits, and the girls at the next table squeal in pleasure, it is hard not to think about slipping out the back door in search of a cab.

"Come on, babe, why don't you come up and have a dance?"

It is past eleven now, and I can see by Brad's jumbo-size grin and eighties' dance moves that he has coaxed the bartender into opening the top shelf bourbon.

"No thanks, darl," I say, in the hope he will go away. "I'll just sit and watch."

As he grooves over and pulls his cousin onto the dance floor, I roll my eyes and pray for a blackout.

"Oh, please!" I beg. "We have already said goodbye to Uncle John twice. Can't we just go?"

"Just one more minute, babe, I promise."

As Brad and his mum begin another round of hugs, kisses, and promises of keeping in touch, I stifle a scream.

September 27

I wake up with a throbbing head, an aching back and doubts about whether or not it was me who had drunk the bar dry the night before. Hearing Brad moan, I roll onto my side and rub my stomach. *No one is getting out of this bed for a while!*

I lie quietly for a while, in the hope of drifting back to sleep. But then Brad starts talking, and I am fully awake.

"You don't look the best," he comments, reaching for his water bottle. "I think we should spend the day on the couch, so you can recoup your strength."

Sure darling, so nice of you to think of me.

September 29

There must be at least a dozen songs that sing the woes of the start of the working week, and this morning I can relate to them all.

"What's the blue-tongue lizard impression for?" Brad asks, reaching past me for his toothbrush.

Closing my mouth, I turn from the mirror. "I don't know. Maybe just Monday-itis."

September 30

I rummage through my handbag hoping to find some loose cold and flu tablets. Pulling out old pens and wrinkled tissues I throw them onto my desk. I want to cry. *How can I have the flu? I have been so careful. It just isn't fair.*

Determined to stop the sickness in its tracks, I keep looking. But after emptying half the contents of my bag, without success, I give up hope. I begin shoving everything back, when something shiny catches my eye. *There you are.* Relieved I reach for my water bottle. I have just begun removing the tablets outer protective layers, when a terrible thought pops into my head. *Oh no, I can't take over-the-counter drugs. Damn it!*

Dropping the now useless pills into the bin, I vow to hunt down Nick and all his horrible, disease-ridden family and friends.

7.00 pm

I hear the familiar sounds of the laundry door opening and keys hitting the bench. Brad is home.

"Where are you darl?" His voice is gruff, and barely resonates above a whisper.

"In here," I call from the living room.

Sticking his head around the corner he says, "Not you too!"

October 1

I am hot. Sweat is dripping from my brow. My eyelashes ache and my body screams for sleep. Across the room a snappy jingle promises to cure my woes in a matter of seconds—all I need to do is swallow two tiny little pills. Remembering the tablets I binned only a few days ago, I throw a pile of crumbled tissues at the TV. "Soldier on with this!" I cry at the rosy-cheeked face smiling back at me.

I hope you are enjoying your honeymoon, Nick!

October 2

Hoping to relieve the pain in my ribs, I am strewn face first across an ottoman. Surrounded by disregarded tissues, I look like the loser in a snowball fight. I have been wallowing in my own self-pity for about an hour when I hear shuffling footsteps. Pleased at the prospect of company, I bolt upright. Brad is standing in the dining room, his familiar tall frame leaning against the table. He looks tired, his tousled dark hair making his face look pale.

I watch him, as he gazes at the clock on the wall.

"How long have you..." he begins.

I start to answer, but before a single word can escape my lips, a deep rattle resonates from his chest, followed by a loud hacking cough. Cringing at its ferocity, I open my mouth to say something comforting, but instead of sympathy, I only join in his misery.

Hunched over and wheezing, the pressure building in my chest is overwhelming. My womb feels like it is about to burst through my ribcage. As my lungs try to force out the poison within, tears well. Recognising that the floodgates are about to open, Brad reacts, and quickly. Within seconds he is across the room, his arms are around me. I want to curse the heavens in frustration and misery. But instead I lean back and let the tears fall.

That afternoon...

I can feel the virus pulsating through my veins. It seems alive. I can feel it tearing down my healthy cells, determined to build an army. I know a major offensive is imminent. I can feel its rage, its hatred for me. I can't imagine the havoc it is reaping inside my body and what it is doing to my unborn child. The fear I feel for my baby is raw, real, unfaltering. It is like facing off with the dark dead eyes of a great white shark. The fear I have for my daughter's safety is primal. It has me on the phone demanding an appointment with my doctor that afternoon. I don't care how busy his morning has been!

October 5

Eyes, they say, are the window to the soul, and as I stare into the two shiny baby browns looking back at me, I search their depths for answers.

There is so much I want to know. So much, I need to be clarified. Will I have the strength to adapt, to grow, to become the person I need to be? Can I do it without losing the person I am? And what about becoming a parent? Will I be a good mum? Will I enjoy my new life?

As the sun bounces off the mirror in front of me, I wait for an answer, but alas, all it shows me is that it needs cleaning.

October 8

I am sitting on a hard blue chair in my obstetrician's office. The clock on the wall appears to be asleep on the job, so to pass the time I pick up a nearby photo album. Flicking through the pages I am treated to dozens of pictures of tired new mothers, and serene faced babies. From the look of some of the hairdos, the album spans a couple of decades. Reaching the last page, I place it back on the table and wander over to the water cooler to top up my drink bottle. I am just tightening the cap, when I hear Dr Whelan behind me. "Come on through."

Without hesitation, I stride towards her office.

"So how have you been?" she enquires, pointing to the seat across from her.

"I have had the flu," I reply grimly, "and it's been pretty bad."

"Let's skip straight to the heartbeat check then?" she smiles knowingly.

"Oh yes, please!" I reply, already standing.

Ba boom! Ba boom! Ba boom!

The sound is like a slot machine hitting the jackpot.

"You can relax." She smiles, "Your baby is doing fine. She is perfectly safe."

Still not convinced, I ask about the infection and the fevers.

Realising I need more, she imparts some useful knowledge, "Well, the body uses all its protective power to keep the baby safe. So, unfortunately, the mum is usually left all but defenceless. You will get better, it will just take a few weeks."

I walk out of the room, damning Mother Nature.

October 9

I am in the kitchen, making breakfast, when I notice something. I can smell cinnamon. Lifting my Maxwell and Williams bowl to my nose I take a big whiff. *Finally!* Laughing out loud, I snort three or four big swigs of heavenly oxygen.

Clearing looking for an explanation, Brad looks up from his newspaper.

"I can breathe again," I whoop.

Chuckling, he shakes his head. "That's great darl."

October 11

It is 2.00 am, and I have been clock watching for the past three hours. The red illuminated numbers beside me provide evidence that a mere fourteen minutes have passed since I last looked their way. Hoping to induce a visit from the Sandman, I fluff my pillows, reposition my body and close my eyes. *Right, now off to sleep with you.*

The beating in my chest begins to slow and my breath deepens. I start to drift off. But then, gravity takes over and I feel myself rolling backwards. "Not again," I grunt bashing the dislodged pillows into place.

Frustrated and tired I look back towards the clock. Okay. If I can get to sleep in the next fifteen minutes, I will get four and a half hours.

Hoping that will be enough, I close my eyes and start counting. One sheep jumps over the fence. Two sheep jump over the fence. Three sheep jump over the … oh no, now I need to pee!

October 15

Okay, Mother Nature, I have a bit of a bone to pick with you. Why would you give me a nine-month break from period pain only to replace it with these awful practice contractions instead?

I am very, very disappointed in you. And considering that you have just ruined one of the only upsides of being pregnant, I am considering changing your name to *Man Nature!*

October 17

"Hey, Im, what's happening?"

Looking up from my computer I see John taking his usual place on my visitor's chair.

"Not much," I reply. "We have the Simple Plan concert tomorrow night, which should be cool."

"I thought that considering *our* taste in music, you were giving concerts a miss?"

"Yeah," I quickly agree. "Most of this summer's line-up has been too rambunctious. But Simple Plan are pretty low key. Hopefully, they shouldn't affect my little music-lover too much."

John looks down at my belly and smiles. "So, are you guys getting a hotel like usual?"

"Absolutely," I reply excitedly, "we have booked a room over-looking the Brisbane River."

"Lucky you, I bet you can't wait to sit on the balcony, drink wine, and take in the view." Pausing, he apologises unnecessarily. "Oh, sorry, forgot you can't drink."

"Doesn't matter. I am just looking forward to doing something other than watching the clock."

October 18

Stepping out of the shower, I am greeted by a one hundred and eighty-degree view of the city. *Wow. It is beautiful up here.* Standing on tiptoes, I lean towards the open window. *Oh, look, there are the botanical gardens. I wonder if you can see the Brisbane Wheel from up here.* Curious, I take a few steps into the lounge.

As hoped the outlook is fantastic. The skyline resembles a diamond mine. I admire the landscape for a few minutes before glancing down towards the river below. A bright light catches my eye and I look towards the hotel adjacent to us. On a balcony, two floors below, a group of twenty-somethings are sitting outside drinking beer. *Oh, to be that young again.*

Out of habit, I reach down to adjust my towel. But instead of poly-cotton, I am greeted with bare flesh. Oh! #@#! No towel. I race to find the curtains. But before my hand touches the cord, I stop. *Humph. If you want to look at the big white naked belly, then go for it.* Giggling at my anti-puritan behaviour I head to the bathroom in search of guest towels. *So this is the "whatever" mummy attitude I have heard so much about.*

Waiting for the concert to start, we are standing in the main foyer of the Brisbane Entertainment Centre.

"Wow!" Brad shouts over the hum of rowdy teenage voices. "We must be the only adults here that aren't babysitting."

"Yeah, I reckon," I reply, suddenly feeling ancient and out of place. "Maybe we should just go hang in the bar; at least it will be quiet."

As we pass the ID checkpoint, the seven-foot security guard doesn't even look our way.

"Do you want a drink?" Brad asks, feeling around for his wallet. "We have time; no one is in the line."

"Sure, lemonade would be sweet."

Two minutes later, as promised, he has returned and we are talking about the latest TV series, to capture our interest—The Sons of Anarchy. We have only been chatting a few minutes, when I notice a stocky middle-aged security guard, heading our way. "Thought you might need this more than me." He smiles, placing a chair beside me.

Feeling helpless and slightly embarrassed, I offer a sincere thank you.

"That was kind," Brad says, watching the guard stroll back to his post.

"Yeah, but now I feel even older and even more out of place than before."

"At least it will help your back."

"I suppose it will," I concede. "Anyway, what do you think Jax is going to say about...?"

Caught up on SAMCRO's latest antics, the time passes quickly and before we know it the first warning siren is wailing. Draining his bourbon, Brad places his glass on a nearby table and picks up my coat. "Well, that's us."

Back in the hotel a few hours later, Brad pours himself a glass of award-winning Margaret River Shiraz and tells me again how amazing I am for getting such good seats. Happy to take the compliment, I smile at my perceived brilliance before getting back to my primary task—enjoying the city lights. I may be sober and have a three-kilo bowling ball attached to my torso, but it is hard not to feel happy. Maybe there is hope for me yet.

October 19

Sunlight falls across my face, instantly reminding me I should have closed the curtains the night before. Too awake to go back to sleep, I reach for my water. I try to be careful but my movement wakes Brad.

He grimaces and rolls my way. "What time is it?"

"Seven-thirty."

"That early." His tone tells me he is not impressed. "What a shame. Anyway, how are you feeling?"

"Pretty good," I reply, stretching my back and climbing out of bed.

"Well, if we are going to be up this early on a Sunday, we may as well go and get some breakfast."

Breakfast before checkout! I muse. *Now that has to be a first.* Usually, we crawl out of bed ten minutes before checkout with bleary eyes and bags to pack. But this morning we are heading down George Street, dressed and watching the city come to life before the big hand reaches eight.

"Want to head to the casino for the morning buffet?" Brad asks, putting his arm around my waist.

"Yeah, sure, their food is always pretty good." At least it is when we hang up our dancing shoes for a pre-dawn fry-up.

Upon arrival, a young brunette, with a distinct British accent leads us to a table beside a large bay window. It is only small but offers a lovely outlook over the plaza. She asks what we want to drink. "A latte (for Brad) and an extra-large cappuccino (for me)," I reply. As we wait for our order, I stare out the window and watch the early risers stride past. Seeing them dressed in coordinated leisure wear instead of 'out to lunch' outfits, makes me realise that this morning's breakfast is just another step in my journey towards a new life.

October 21

"Oh Paige, *please* stop using my bladder as a trampoline!"

Later that evening

"Come on, darl," Brad says, "we're going for a walk."

Pushing the water bottle away, I moan and bury my head under a cushion. "I'm too tired."

Never one to retreat, my beloved tries a new angle. "They say exercise shortens labour."

October 23

Tonight was our first antenatal class. It was both scary and exciting.

Walking into a room filled with other women rubbing their bellies and stretching their backs felt wonderful. Finally, people who understood how I was feeling. We instantly hit it off with another mid-aged couple, Shana and Mani, and even managed a few nervous jokes before the midwife arrived and welcomed us.

"First we will go through the agenda, and then we'll stop for supper before..." The mention of food has all the mums-to-be smiling. As she continues her spiel, I stretch out my legs and settle into my chair. Her voice is calming, its drone instantly putting me at ease.

The first half of the class flies by and before I know it we are standing around the fruit and cheese platters, sipping coffee. Brad, the eternal social butterfly, is talking to a tall slim man wearing a T-shirt featuring the eighties band, The Smiths. They seem to be getting on well, so I leave him to chat while I make a beeline for the sandwiches. Most of the girls are helping themselves to the complimentary snacks, and we get talking straight away. With so much in common there is instant rapport, so when the midwife announces it is time for the tour we are all a little disappointed. Grabbing a few last-minute strawberries, I throw my Styrofoam cup in the bin and follow the line of parents-to-be out the door.

Our first stop is the delivery suites. Walking through the large dark doors into the main corridor, I instantly notice the smell of antiseptic, then the sound of a woman screaming. Hearing her pleas to 'go home', I look towards my new comrades and gulp.

Ignoring what is probably an everyday event in her life, the nurse leads us through another door. "Okay folks, this is one of our delivery suites. The bathroom is through here," she points towards a door at the back of the room. "And once you are in labour, you will have the option of using a birthing ball or leaning ..."

Zoning out, I take in my surroundings. Looking at the faded rose coloured walls, and eighties décor, it is hard to imagine the room is designed for anything but hosting my grandma's crochet group. As I look from the dated landscape paintings to the faces of my new friends, I am quickly reminded of why we are here. Seeing their darting eyes and ashen complexions, I know I am not the only one feeling scared.

"And these are the forceps we use when ...."

Hearing a word that has been haunting me for months instantly drags my attention back to the nurse. She is holding what looks like a large set of metals tongs, and as I consider their implication my shoulders shudder.

In front of me, Elaine's response is similar, and I watch sympathetically as she sways on her feet and reaches for her husband's shoulder. She is unaware that the movement has caused her perfectly groomed ginger hair to become tangled in the straps of her Gucci knock-off.

Feeling ill, I search for a quick exit. Glancing towards the open door, I notice more than one set of eyes looking the same way. I want to run out of the room and hide somewhere safe but before I can Brad's strong hand wraps around mine. Feeling comforted, I look up, to see his best, but still somewhat unconvincing, "It will be okay" smile.

October 25

My aches and pains are getting worse, both in their intensity and their frequency. Even simple acts, like getting dressed or climbing in and out of the car, have become involved, and leave me breathless. My legs and calves ache all the time. And thanks to being woken every twenty minutes by aching hips, I don't remember what sleep is. Life is so annoying at the moment, I could just scream.

And if the exhaustion wasn't enough, I now have the inevitable weight gain to deal with. To date, I have put on ten kilograms and I hate it! I feel fat, heavy, and very unattractive. I can't even shave my legs or paint my toenails. I feel like a big fat hairy frump!

October 29

I can't believe it is finally here—trimester three. Two down and one to go! It is like getting a whiff of the weekend on a dreary Thursday afternoon.

And even though I am very excited to finally be here, I can't begin to describe how long this pregnancy is taking. I feel like I have been pregnant for five years, at least! I cannot remember life before becoming pregnant. I feel like I am stuck in a bad dream where I am on a road with no end.

October 30

Tonight is antenatal night. The classes are being held at Auchen-flower, five minutes from work, but a good hour's round trip from home. Not wanting to spend all night in the car, I call Brad.

"Hey, darl. I thought we should meet for dinner before class."

"Great idea. Where were you thinking?"

"Arrivederci's."

"Of course!" He laughs. "I'll meet you there around six."

Satisfied, I hang up the phone and get back to work.

Stuffed with garlic-laden pizza, we head to the hospital. As soon as we enter the room, we spot Jemma and Dave and plonk ourselves in the empty seats beside them. Without hesitation, the boys shake hands and begin discussing the latest cricket scores. Used to spending the summer as sports widows, Jemma and I roll our eyes and head to the food table, chatting the whole way.

"I am exactly the same." She nods sympathetically. "It is driving me crazy."

We continue comparing notes until Brad interrupts us with news that the midwife has arrived.

She drops her handbag by the whiteboard, grabs a pen and writes two big words in red. The act has an instant quietening effect on the room.

"Hi, everyone, glad you could all make it. Tonight we are going to spend some time discussing pain relief."

Looking out at her attentive listeners, she begins walking us through some of the gentler options available to us.

"When is she getting to the epidural?" Jemma whispers. "That's all I'm interested in."

"Me too," I reply in a little voice.

"And me," Shana murmurs from the next chair.

Facing forward we feign interest until she reaches our topic of interest.

"Now this is the equipment the anaesthetist uses."

As a giant steel syringe begins its rounds, warm smiling faces turn sallow and pasty. When the catheter finally reaches my lap, I hold it limply in my hand and sigh deeply. *There goes any thought of being saved by a knight in shining armour.*

November 4

Today is one of my favourite Champagne events: The Melbourne Cup—the infamous horse race that stops a nation. Like most people in this Great Southern Land, I look forward to the Cup, in particular, the long boozy lunch that accompanies it. But today, for the first time in spring carnival history, I am swapping an afternoon of cold chicken and sweepstakes for aromatherapy and a massage table.

Hopping on the table, the masseuse asks if I have any areas of concern.

Turning my head, I unload, "My back, hips, shoulders. Oh, and I have had some trouble with my sciatic nerve too."

"Does it hurt when you walk?"

"Yes, and getting in and out of bed."

"No worries. I'll see what I can do."

As the sweet smell of lavender fills my airways, the hold on my eyelids weaken, and I drift away.

An hour later, I walk out of the wellness centre feeling like I have just picked the Cup winner ... well, nearly.

November 14

The 444 is crawling up Moggill Road. I am sitting in my usual spot, by the window, and thanks to the familiarity of the passing houses my mind is blank. Dozens of colours and shapes pass before me, but I take little notice. I am tired, and the constant rocking and drone of a road well travelled keeps me in a tranquil state. I can smell the cologne of the man sitting behind me, and hear the muffled sound of music from the school children in front. All is well with the world, and I allow my eyelids to close.

Then, all of a sudden the peace is broken. I feel like I have been sucker-punched. My body is forced into a front-facing foetal position. Panting like a dog on a hot summer's day, I dare not move. Three more contractions follow in quick succession. The pain is akin to a burn. Logic tells me to call out to the driver, but, then all at once like a passing tornado, the ferocity is gone, and all is calm.

Feeling like I have just been slapped, and hard, I focus on returning to my serene state. But, peace is not yet on the cards. Within seconds, the eye of the storm passes and an explosion ignites within. It feels like my skeleton is trying to escape its bonds with relentless determination. For a while, I float along in a river of pain, lost to the world.

"Are you okay?"

Fighting the calamity in my head, I tune into the voice beside me. Looking up I see a middle-aged woman leaning over me, wisps of blonde hair falling around her ears. She looks worried.

Not wanting to cause this guardian angel in blue any concern, I take a deep breath and force a smile. "Don't worry. I'm not in labour; it is just cramps."

"Glad to hear." She smiles, patting my arm. "You take care, and please let me know if you need anything."

As her black four-inch heels carry her back to her seat, I hear a loud sigh of relief coming from the direction of the driver's seat.

November 16

As the end of the year draws closer, the reality of my situation begins to set in. I am going to be a mother. This is actually real. Not a temp job. Not a favour for a friend. This is going to be permanent. No one but me is going to be making decisions about this new little person. I am going to be the CEO of this new and fragile life, and it is going to be forever! I am forty-nine per cent excited and fifty-one per cent terrified!

November 17

This morning our tech support manager, Lina, dropped in to say hello.

"Wow," she says sympathetically, noticing my bright red cheeks, "you really must be struggling with this heat."

"Yeah, I sure am," I moan. "And they say it's going to be a super-hot summer this year."

"Maybe I should bring in the grandkids' plastic pool so we can take turns ladling you with cold water."

I laugh in agreement. Typical marine biologist ... always trying to save the poor beached whale.

November 21

I am really starting to feel pregnant now. You know, the type of pregnant you see in the movies. I don't know if it is just the pregnancy getting me down, but I am still having doubts about becoming a mother. Every day I still wonder about what our life is going to be like after the baby is born, and whether or not we have made the right decision. At the same time though, I already love Paige so much that I wouldn't give her up for the world. I suppose it could just be nerves caused by all the changes in my life, but still I wonder.

November 27

This week Queensland lived through the worst storm season in over twenty-five years. It has been quite frightening. Tonight as we waited for our antenatal class to start, we sat in the hospital's foyer watching the six o'clock news on their oversized TV.

A reporter in a lemon coloured blouse and pin striped skirt came into view and moved a large microphone to her lips. "Last night, a heavily pregnant woman was cut off from the hospital by flood-waters in the Gold Coast hinterland..."

What!

It seems that the woman lived on the city's country fringes, and whilst on the way to the hospital had been cut off by floodwaters. With creeks rising on both sides and nowhere to turn, she and her husband battled across a dark field seeking help at a nearby farmhouse. As the storm raged outside, she huddled down with strangers. And with no chance of a helicopter rescue, gave birth to a healthy baby boy thanks to the medical advice she received over the couple's walkie-talkies.

Transfixed by the screen, her plight began unfolding in my mind. I could easily imagine her staggering through the mud, hair soaking wet, dress plastered to her swollen belly, tears running down her face as she frantically fought to reach the dim light in the distance. Wild rain, howling wind and lightning cracking all around her, I pictured her stumbling along, praying for her life and that of her unborn child. It was just so scary.

Later in class, the story was on everybody's minds. And when an enormous bolt of lightning cracked outside the window, Elaine turned straight towards Shana and me and whispered, "I pray I don't end up like that lady on the news."

"Me too!" we both replied in quick succession.

But with the wind shrieking around the building like a banshee, the likelihood of something equally terrible happening seemed a distinct possibility.

November 28

The countdown is on. I now only have two weeks left at work. I am very excited but have just realised how much I need to do before I go. Usually I am only organising for someone to cover me for a couple of weeks of annual leave, but this time, I will be gone for over a year. The realness is a little overwhelming.

When I started this job, I was given a desk, a computer, and an empty canvas. It has taken years to get things running smoothly, to turn a neglected role into an essential one. Having put so much effort in, I am apprehensive that it may all come undone. Delegating is not one of my strong points, so I am finding it quite difficult to let go.

December 1

I told Brad I was doing some last minute shopping today but instead I am standing in line at Gloria Jean's coffee, waiting to order.

I am daydreaming and taking in the sights and sounds, when a young blond lad, resembling a seventies front-man, asks me what I would like.

"Regular decaf cappuccino," I reply, glancing down at the tattoo on his wrist. Wow, I remember when you couldn't show your ink at work. I must be getting old.

"That will be four-eighty, thanks."

After handing over my money, I step to one side.

The centre is buzzing with chatter, and as I survey the hustle and bustle around me, I notice a group of twenty-somethings on my left wearing spray-on jeans, ballet flats, and perfectly fitting t-shirts. Watching as they flick their pencil straight hair and swipe their diamante-covered smartphones, I feel a pang of envy. *I will never be that thin or that carefree ever again.*

December 4

Work is a buzz with tomorrow's Christmas party. Our end-of-year function is one of the university's biggest and most highly anticipated events, and now that I have decided not to attend, I am feeling a bit left out.

It is hard to fathom that this year I won't be getting half sloshed on the undergrads' cocktail mix. I won't be playing wheelbarrows, winning the egg and spoon race, or jumping on the inflated castle. I won't even get the chance to co-host the very naughty but very amusing annual Christmas awards. Overall, I am feeling very un-Christmassy. For the first time ever I can totally relate to Mr Scrooge.

December 5

Whilst my excitement builds as my big day draws near, the journey for others is just beginning. I am in the middle of folding a basket of freshly dried clothes when I hear the phone ringing. It is Abbey.

"Hey, sis, how are you?"

"Actually," she moans back, "I am feeling really sick."

"Oh no," I reply, slightly worried, "that's terrible. What's wrong?"

"Well, it's not too terrible." She laughs. "I am pregnant!"

I jump up and down with excitement, though my feet don't leave the floor.

"Oh, that is awesome!" I reply. "Who would have thought that two thirty-something sisters would end up pregnant at the same time?"

"I know, it is weird," she agrees. "What a shame we live in different states. It would have been fun, waddling around the baby stores together, bitching, moaning and eating chocolate."

December 8

Today was a reality check. For months, I have been trying to focus only on the positives of motherhood. But after two hours at our local shopping centre watching frazzled mothers in thrown-together outfits wrestling tired two-year-olds having tantrums, I am freaking out! I can't stop thinking that I have made the wrong decision. I can't stop thinking that I am going to be trapped in some alternate lifestyle, a lifestyle in which I am at the mercy of a poorly behaved toddler. A lifestyle in which I will be a dishevelled, yoghurt-covered mess and too tired to care!

December 9

After spending the morning plotting next year's workflow chart, I take a well-deserved break. With only a few days left until my leave starts, I need to do some packing. I begin by pulling down Christmas decorations, then move onto my personal items. As I fill two small archive boxes with my worldly possessions, I feel a strange sense of loss. This space has been my office and my sanctuary for such a long time and without my personal touches it looks bare and clinical. It looks like it did on the first day I got the keys. Work has never been my favourite place to be but all of a sudden the thought of leaving my little fish bowl saddens me.

December 10

Arriving at the Staff Club for my farewell lunch, I am pleased to find most of my colleagues have come along to say goodbye. Our party occupies two long tables situated on the deck. In the middle of the one closest to me, I spy a bunch of flowers, an enormous pile of gifts, and an empty chair. Taking a seat, I feel humbled. "Wow, guys, this is too much."

"You deserve it, Im," Selena calls from the end of my table. "Now hurry up and start opening."

Piling adorable little blankets, matching outfits, and an array of baby paraphernalia, on the chair behind me, I look up to see a familiar face. It is Sue, my usual boss, who is currently off on her second bout of maternity leave. Catching my eye, she smiles and comes straight over. She takes a seat opposite me. As she places her bag on the table, I look over her shoulder and take in the view of the campus lakes. Watching the light reflect off the water, the memory of a long-distant conversation we once had begins to surface.

"What are you smirking at?" Sue asks, reaching for the menu.

"Oh, just remembering that Christmas Eve, when we sat here sipping champagne, soaking up the sunshine and—"

"Talking about how we were never getting married or having kids," she interjects, with a laugh. "Who would have ever guessed?"

December 11

It is day one of my maternity leave.

The dictionary describes maternity leave as a noun: a leave of absence for an expectant or new mother for the birth and care of a baby.

I describe it as: a period of deserved rest. A point in time, where a woman partially resembling a bloated Barbie doll, sits on a couch, reads magazines, and eats candy, all whilst giving the kettle, and TV remote a good workout.

December 12

My to-do list is long enough to rival Santa's good list. I wonder how I ever found time to go to work.

Later that day

Brad walks in, puts down his satchel, and heads straight for the tissue box.

Looks like our sickness woes aren't over for the year just yet.

December 14

A bright light pushes against my eyelids, forcing me to ascend from my dark world. But the moment my room comes into view, I regret my decision. Something just isn't right. The light is searing my eyes, and despite the air conditioner being on, I feel clammy. Suspecting the worst, I swallow. My throat burns, and I feel a pinching sensation in my ears. Moaning, as if it will make any kind of difference, I reach for my water bottle. *Damn you universe!*

December 16

For months, it has felt like I have been operating as two separate selves, with both parts demanding a harmonious existence despite their opposing natures.

There is one self, the part I have lived, cried and laughed with for as long as I can remember, trying to function as normal. It is the part that chats with friends over lunch, shouts at the football ref, and cranks up Motley Crue when I am alone in the car. It is the part that I think of as me. But, there is also a new self fighting for recognition, a part that is screaming to be heard, a self which know things are changing, a self that is trying to accept that life as we know it is over—that it is time to change. It is the part that knows we will soon be buying low heels instead of low cut. It is a persistent little bugger, and I am not yet sure we are friends.

December 17

I am feeling very fragile today ... like a thin piece of glass that could easily break. Being sick and unable to do anything to help myself has taken me to a whole new low. What is making this pregnancy so difficult is not just the weariness of a particular day but the accumulation of months and months of tiredness. And, even though I am surrounded by people offering compassion and support, sometimes it just isn't enough. Sometimes everything just catches up with me, and I feel entirely alone and overwhelmed. Some days I feel out of my depth. I feel misplaced. I know deep down that women have been doing this for thousands of years and have survived but on days like today, it seems like I am the first and only one.

December 18

I answer the phone. It is Mum.

"How are you going, sweetheart?" she asks.

"I'm okay," I say even though it is only partially correct. "I am just feeling big, fat, and useless!"

"I know," she replies sympathetically. "It's really hard carrying through summer. Are you still keeping up your walks?"

"I'm trying to but I am so uncomfortable. And it feels like the baby is going to fall out at any moment."

I wait for a reply but there is only silence. I check I haven't accidently hung up the phone, but then I hear my mother's sweet, warm laughter. "You should be so lucky!"

December 23

It feels like Paige is planning a trip, perhaps moving house. I can feel her busying herself inside. As she pushes unseen items from one side of my belly to the other, I feel like a character from a Ridley Scott film. One of those poor, helpless victims from the *Alien* series who after realising they are infected by a fast gestating parasite, can do nothing but wait in dread for the moment their abdomen will inevitably explode.

December 24

Santa Claus is coming tonight and, even though I am not feeling particularly festive, I attempt to muster some Christmas spirit. As I wander round the house trying to busy myself, I try not to focus on the things that hurt—my back, my feet, my hips. But despite my efforts I only manage to distract myself in short bursts. Feeling deflated and full of self- pity, I head to my office to fire up the PC.

Bigmumma is online and unloading furiously. "Not feeling very festive at the moment. So over this pregnancy. Just want this baby out!"

Mumof2 agrees. "All I want to do is sleep. So sick of hearing everyone talk about how great Christmas is going to be this year."

Scrolling through the confessions of my fellow inmates, it becomes clear I am not alone in my yuletide misery. Women from Sydney to Perth and from the US to the UK are all shouting the same mantra: *Bah! Humbug!*

2.00 pm

After peeking through the kitchen blinds and seeing blue skies, I head to my room in search of bathers. On my way, I call out to Brad but get no reply.

Stepping into the deliciously cold water of my backyard swimming pool is heavenly. Sinking into its depths I feel like a model for the latest luxury bubble bath commercial. Sure, I may not be surrounded by rose petals and lavender but the effect of instantly becoming fifty kilos lighter is enough to put a look of ecstasy on my face.

Leaning back I bask in the warmth of the sun. With the water embracing me from all sides, I feel like I am in another world—a world where I no longer hurt, a world where I am the only thing that matters. Separating from the hustle and bustle of modern life, I begin to relax. Time drifts away like smoke on the wind.

I am lost in this new world, when a voice calls me back from my dream state.

"Are you going to stay in there all day?" Brad shouts from the back door.

Looking up, I grin cheekily. "Well, I would if I had something to do. Like, say, drink icy cold beer."

December 25

"Merry Christmas," Brad mumbles, reaching my way.

"You too!" I answer, returning his hug.

In no hurry to get out of bed, we lie in a mass of pillows and stare into space. This year is partners Christmas, which means our families are away and we are on our own. With only the two of us, I expect the day to be pretty uneventful but still want it to feel like a holiday, so after a while decide to get up and make a start on a hot three-course breakfast.

"Something smells good," Brad says walking into the kitchen, freshly showered and dressed.

"All your favourites. It shouldn't be too long."

Picking up the crystal glass sitting at his usual place setting, he looks my way.

"Bringing out the good stuff, eh?"

"Yep!" I reply, popping a bottle of non-alcoholic Edenvale Cuvée. "If I am going to have a Clayton's breakfast, I want to enjoy the bubbles."

After a lazy morning, I decide it is time to get outside and enjoy the sunshine. I ask Brad if he would like some cheese and crackers by the pool and he jumps at the idea.

Five minutes later, laden with glasses, an ice bucket and a tray of freshly chopped deli delights, we step out of the house and into a furnace. I can feel the heat burning the soles of my feet. We instantly retreat back into our artificial winter. Not prepared to suffer the sweltering conditions outside, we spend the afternoon scaring ourselves silly with back-to-back horror movies.

December 26

For the first time in years, I welcome Boxing Day in, without a hangover. For us, December twenty-six usually revolves around two things: watching test cricket and celebrating my sister Amanda's birthday.

"It certainly feels weird watching the game here and not down at the pub," Brad says, reaching for the remote.

"Yeah, just you, me and the bump," I reply, taking a seat next to him on the couch. "It's hardly comparable to our usual post-Christmas pastimes of drinking beer and eating leftovers."

Nodding in agreement, Brad finds the sports channel. "And don't forget stuffing ourselves with mud cake, and dancing to dawn in Melbas."

December 28

I wake at dawn but it takes a further three hours to drag myself out of bed. *I really hope Paige isn't a morning person.*

December 30

Peering over the latest copy of *WHO* magazine, I look down at my legs, precariously balancing on the edge of my black leather-look ottoman. *It's official. I have fankles.*

December 31

Closing my magazine, I turn to Brad "What a way to bring in the New Year, stuck at home reading celebrity news."

"Well, we don't have to stay here. The coast is only an hour away. Why don't you give Tori and Dean a call?"

After a couple of hours of drinking beer by the pool at Tori and Dean's—well some of us—the maxi taxi arrives. We head off to the relative safety of the Mermaid Beach Surf Club so the boys can gorge on seafood whilst the girls chat. Grabbing a table with water views, we have soon settled in and, before I know it, the boys are finishing their second bottle of Cab Sav and the clock is inching towards midnight.

"Hey, sis, do you want to go home?" Tori asks. "You look uncomfortable."

"It's okay," I fib, as I fiddle in my chair. "Let's wait for the fireworks."

Shouting over the music, Tori rounds up the boys. "Come on, grab your glasses, we're heading outside."

Leaning against the veranda rail, a warm summer breeze blows against my bare arms. I can smell the salt in the air, and hear the faint sound of waves crashing. As we wait for the year that was 2008 to end, we place ridiculous looking paper hats on our heads and ready ourselves for the countdown.

"Five, four, three, two, one..."

An explosion of colour fills the sky. Tori blows her whistle, and we shout, "Happy New Year!" to the masses of party-goers scattered across the golden sand below.

With toasts made and the last of the party favours popped, Brad looks at his watch and suggests going home. More than ready to swap designer lycra for practical cotton, I nod in agreement. Draining our drinks, we make a quick pit stop before heading downstairs in search of the courtesy bus.

"What do you mean it left twenty minutes ago?" Tori growls. "You knew we were booked in for the home trip."

The doorman, a baby-faced lad who looks barely out of high school, had been left with the job of informing twenty or so tired and somewhat intoxicated revellers that they have no way of getting home. Standing in the dimly lit car park, with his sandy hair blowing across his eyes, I almost feel sorry for him.

He begins like they always do, by offering an indifferent apology.

The father-to-be who is completely over the apathetic attitudes of strangers takes over from my sister. "We were told to meet here at quarter past twelve."

"Well, yes that was the plan," the young man says, "but the driver wanted to get a jump on the traffic."

Closing my eyes, I take a deep breath. I need to calm myself down. All I want to do is wrap my puffy red fingers around the young pup's neck and squeeze. *Why would a courtesy bus leave five minutes before midnight?* I shake my head in disbelief. *And why didn't they warn us?*

Realising that having a grievous bodily harm charge hanging over my head would probably not be the ideal way to begin motherhood, I suggest looking for a cab. Stranded and sullen we start our trek towards the main road.

As expected the Gold Coast highway is littered with people calling it a night or heading out in the pursuit of more fun.

"Push your stomach out further," Dean suggests with a laugh.

Our plan to secure a ride seems to hold merit at first but after two hours on the side of a steamy noisy road, it becomes apparent that compassion isn't on the cards tonight. As we watch another black and white cab full of larking merrymakers zoom past, Tori shows her frustration, by stamping her feet. "That's it!" she yells, walking closer to the curb. "The next one is stopping."

Seeing a taxi approach, she jumps out onto the road with no regard for her personal safety. Waving her arms like a maniac, she screams at the slowing driver, "My sister is in labour, you have to help us!"

As her intended target rolls down the passenger-side window, she turns to us with a triumphant smile. "Come on. It's working."

But her joy is short lived, as it soon becomes apparent that the driver's real intention is only to slow down long enough to hurl abuse her way. But Tori, not one to shy away from a challenge, ignores the threat of a scolding and pushes her face against the window and projects her voice, "Please. You can't just leave us here!"

Luck is finally on our side and, after faking contractions in the back seat of a 2005 Ford Fairlane for a solid five minutes, Tori is letting us in through her front door.

Collapsing onto the couch, Dean says, "You two are terrible."

Tori grins. "Yes, but we're home."

January 2

I used to own a pair of cheap bathroom scales; you know the type you buy from K-mart for ten dollars, the ones that rattle when you stand on them, and give you a three-way bet on their accuracy. But since becoming serious about looking after my health I upgraded to the deluxe digital model. My bathroom now sports a shiny Tanita BC541 Innerscan. The set of scales is so high-tech they can tell me in a matter of seconds whether I am my real age of thirty-six or if my behaviour over the last week has me more tightly pegged at a desirable twenty-five or a horrifying fifty-three.

Unfortunately, today's love-hate relationship has spiralled straight to the hate end of the spectrum. Today my shiny silver gadget is telling me I am at the high end of the average pregnancy weight gain. I want to put an end to this smug torture device but considering its price tag, I simply growl and stomp out of the room.

January 4

With Brad back at work and no one to keep me company, I have spent the morning being domestic.

Yum! Homemade scones for afternoon tea. Lucky me! Setting the timer to fifteen, I head outside armed with a basket of wet clothes.

Placing two pegs onto an adorable little pinafore, I begin humming. *Oh! A hand-embroidered ladybug ... these clothes are just too cute!* Reaching into the basket, I feel like a goody-two-shoes sixties housewife. But despite myself, I am happy. This life may be noticeably different to the one I am used to but it doesn't feel that horrible either. In fact, I don't really mind it much at all.

Hearing the postman's bike outside, I grab the keys. *Awesome! Something to do!* I clamber down the front stairs as best I can and spot a package sitting behind the letterbox. *Double awesome!*

I race inside and rip it open, even though I know what's inside. My TENS machine—an electronic pain-relief device. Flipping through the instructions I mutter to myself. *I hope this baby works.*

Pain management has undeniably been a number-one priority for me. I don't think a day has passed when I haven't wondered about pushing a baby out. Me? The girl who cries over a splinter and faints at the first sign of blood! As images of spurting red liquid enter my mind, I focus on the blooming gardenias outside and begin chanting my new mantra, "It is only one day. It is only one day."

January 5

I wake up and look at the clock. It's 10.13 am. My internal calculator switches on. *About three hours.*

Getting up I wander into the kitchen. I must look a treat because the first thing Brad does when he looks at me, is to click on the kettle.

"So what time did you get to sleep?" he asks, reaching for an empty mug.

"About seven, I think."

"That sucks. Rest is so important for you right now."

"Yeah, I know. I just don't get it, if my body is so tired, why doesn't it sleep?"

Later that day

Taking the sample jar from my hand, my doctor gestures towards the examination table located on her left. Knowing the routine well, I jump up and stick out my arm.

"It looks like your blood pressure is up a bit," she muses, unfastening the arm tapes.

"Of course it is up," I joke nervously. "I am going to have a baby in a few weeks."

She smiles back. "Yes, but we will need to keep an eye on it."

"Okay."

"Oh, and we'll need some blood work."

Oh great! I think as I slide my swollen feet into my thongs. I am already feeling emotional and scared. Now more blood tests. Skulking back to the car, I can feel my stress levels rising further. *Stupid blood pressure!*

January 6

Dripping wet I step out of the shower and reach for a towel. Unable to dry myself properly, I pat away a little excess water before putting on my underwear. I am doing my best 'I'm a little tea-pot' impersonation when gravity takes over. *Oh! @#$%, I'm going over.*

Bracing myself for a hard landing my hands fly out, but before I get a close-up of the carpet, I feel Brad's steadying arm. "Here, let me help you with those."

I feel like a complete invalid but welcome his offer anyway. Like it or not, I have had to learn to accept help for a lot of this sort of thing lately. Lucky for me, though, Brad hasn't used the opportunity to make a single wisecrack. This has been a real gracious act for him, particularly since Australian men are notorious for taking a pun anywhere and anytime they can. And it is usually their missus that is first and fairest game.

I am squirming on the couch like a politician at question time when Brad stands, turns off the TV and instructs me to get my shoes.

"Come on, we're going for a walk."

Considering it is after ten, I want to tell him to bugger off but instead, sigh and toddle off to the laundry.

Two minutes later as we step out into the sweltering summer heat, I realise I should have trusted my earlier judgement. Climbing down the stairs, we turn left and head towards the new housing estate at the end of the road.

Within about sixty seconds, Brad, a self-confessed gym junkie, is half way up the street whilst I lag behind clambering for breath.

"Come on, darl," Mr Zoom calls encouragingly. "Just one little loop around the block."

"I'm coming," I yell, with no intention of increasing my speed. Looking up at the hill in front of me, I consider turning around but decide to stop for water instead. I look down towards the bottle in my hand and at that exact moment I realise I am still wearing the hideous discount store nightie I bought for the hospital. Horrified I pick up speed.

January 7

It was no surprise that I fainted at pathology today. My fear of needles is long-standing. When I was five, I prematurely added a few grey hairs to my mother's golden locks, by running away and hiding at the local train tracks after a tetanus shot. Even when I was a little older, and my girlfriends were getting belly-button rings and butterfly tattoos on their ankles, I was happy to display my individuality through killer boots and wild designer outfits.

I have spent my whole adult life, avoiding anything that could cause me pain and injury. I am happy to keep my relationship with scabby knees and grazed elbows a childhood memory. Sure I like to have fun, and enjoy the thrill of a rollercoaster, but if there is any chance I could end up bleeding, I will probably opt out. This, of course, has been okay so far but is going to become a bit of a problem; on the day I have to give birth. But, at this point in time, I have to just hope I can wing it on the day. Somehow I need to become as brave as the little boy I saw running from his blood test, shouting, "Daddy, Daddy, look what I got for being so good".

January 9

Full-term. What an achievement! From now on when people stop me in the shop, I can confidently say, "Any day now."

January 10

One of the nicest things about having a baby is having the opportunity to decorate a nursery. And this morning my plan is to add some last minute touches. As I walk into Paige's room, the room that has hosted many a drunken houseguest, I stop. There right between the pink princess themed curtains is an enormous crack.

Walking closer in order to assess the damage, I know that looking for the culprit is futile—the bird that ruined my day would be long gone by now. As I run my finger over the fresh scar on my newly tinted windows, I sigh at my misfortune. *Twenty-nine windows in the house and my feathered friend had to pick this one.*

January 11

Placing my hand on my belly, I feel Paige wiggling under my fingers and marvel at the miracle that is creating life.

January 14

It's official. Brad and I *will* be parents sometime in the next three weeks. Scary!

January 16

I open my eyes to see Brad's smiling face. "Good morning, Mummy. How are you?"

"Not the best," I whisper. "I feel nauseated and hot."

Frowning, he climbs out of bed. "Maybe I should stay home just in case something happens."

"I'll be okay," I reply, trying to sound confident. "It's not like the baby is just going to pop out. I'll be in labour for hours." *Yep! Hours and hours and hours...*

January 17

It is mind-boggling to think that I am going to have a baby soon. I still feel way too selfish, carefree and uninterested in paper mache to become a mother. It has occurred to me lately that I may just be a little too old and a little too tired, to be entering a world of two-hourly feeds, and twenty minute micro-naps. I have a horrible feeling I am going to feel like the only one who wore sneakers to a black tie event.

January 19

After another night spent staring at the ceiling, I roll over to see if Brad is up. I must have dozed off at some point during the early hours of the morning because he is gone. A quick look at the clock tells me, he has been up for an hour. Thirsty, I reach for my water bottle and notice Brad standing by the edge of the bed dressed in business gear.

"I'm off to work now," he says, leaning over to kiss my cheek. "Make sure you rest up."

I utter something about having a good day, before plunging my face under the doona. Come on powers that be; please let me get some sleep tonight. Please ... please ... please ...

2.00 am

Did no one listen to my prayers?

The thirty-two-hour day

Tuesday January 20

Annoyed that something has woken me, I sit up. The clock tells me it is 3:45 am. *Great,* I think sarcastically, *only an hour has passed. Well, I may as well go to the bathroom now.*

Using the soft glow of the en-suite night-light, I navigate my way through the darkness. When I feel the cold smoothness of tiles under my feet I know I have reached my destination. I walk to the toilet and begin lowering myself. But as soon as I reach the seat, I notice something strange. A warm wet substance is running down my leg. *Yuck! What is that?* Sure it must just be a little 'wee' accident, I mop up the mess before tip-toeing back to bed, with an empty bladder and two bath towels.

Lying back on freshly washed poly-cotton, I can smell fabric softener. Wanting to get back to sleep as soon as possible, I begin using the 'squeeze and relax' technique, I learnt at ante-natal. After fifteen minutes it is evident that, not only am I no closer to returning to the land of nod, but my lower body is drenched. *What is going on?*

I get out of bed and open the second drawer of my duchess in search of dry pyjamas, then panic and excitement washes over me. *Oh my God! My waters have broken! I am in labour!*

Feeling silly standing in the dark doing nothing, I head to the kitchen. My mind is racing as I walk down the hallway. *OMG! This means I am going to have a baby—today!* Blood courses through my veins. Aimlessly I wander around the kitchen like a person who is only at the mall to escape the summer heat. I pour myself a glass of water and with no idea what to do next, head back to my room to clear away the soiled towels.

I roll the first one into a ball before reaching for its twin, but quickly realise the corner is lodged under Brad's shoulder. Trying not to disturb my sleeping partner, I give the towel a gentle tug. It moves quickly, but the action wakes Brad. Turning my way he rubs his face. "What's up? Are you okay?"

"Yeah, I'm all right," I reply excitedly. "My waters just broke."

"Okay, then," he mumbles, before rolling back into his original position.

For a moment I stand perplexed but then the soon to be daddy leaps out of bed like a jack-in-the-box. "Your waters broke!" he yells madly. "That means you're in labour, doesn't it? Oh my God! What do we do?"

"Don't worry," I reply, sounding calmer than I really am. "Nothing is going to happen yet."

Pulling on a shirt he bounds to the kitchen, switching on all the lights as he goes. Laughing at his antics, I pick up the phone and dial the hospital. After talking to a midwife for a few minutes, I hang up and turn to Brad. He is filling the kettle.

"So what did she say?" he demands.

"Well, she wants us there in the next hour or so."

"Okay, that's fine. You go finish packing and I'll make you a cuppa."

Happy for the distraction, I head to my room. Taking my hospital checklist in my hands, I begin humming the words to Jimmy Hendrix's Purple Haze. When Brad arrives with my tea, I am still rooted in the same position. Handing me the cup, with the advice that it is hot, he races out of the room with no apparent purpose.

Seeking some normality, I take a sip. The steaming liquid scolds my tongue but the pain helps bring me back to reality. Feeling more grounded I begin throwing a few random items into my toiletry bag before turning around to see the room filling with light.

For years, this enormous star in the sky has shone on this world. To this giant star, today is no different to any other it has witnessed in the last few millennia. But today is different, today the breaking of dawn heralds my daughter's birthday and the beginning of our new life. Not wanting to miss the magnitude of the moment, I stop what I am doing. I want every detail to be sewn into my memory forever. But my serenity is soon shattered by Brad's urgent voice.

"Come on, darl. We've got to go."

"I'm coming," I reply. "I'm just zipping up my bag now."

"Just leave it," he calls out frantically. "I'll get it. Just grab the camera so we can take a quick photo by the pool."

Five minutes later, the proof that I was once the size of a small island is captured and I am sitting in the passenger seat of our blood red Toyota Camry. The day is dawning and the world feels quiet and desolate. For once luck is on our side and the notorious Moggill Road is all but empty, its usual inhabitants still deliberating between toast and cereal. As we watch soon to be opened curtains race by us, any thoughts of giving birth in the back seat are quickly diminished and we arrive at the hospital without incident.

Entering through the main doors, people happy to be witnessing such a special moment, look at us and smile. Not wanting to appear rude, I muster a happy face in response. From the outside I may seem calm, but inside I am freaking out!

Noticing my swollen belly and overnight bag, the receptionist beams, finishes her call and points towards the nearest lifts. Pressing the button marked three, the doors close, and we are soon travelling upwards to the place where our lives will change forever. As the lift bell dings, we step out onto blue patterned carpet, nervous but excited. We have only taken a few steps when I hear a friendly voice beside me.

"Ah! Here for the delivery suite. Follow me."

The nurse walks us down the now familiar hall and leads us into suite five, the room we visited on our first visit to the hospital. Upon entering the room, she points towards the bag rack before handing me a blue gingham birthing robe.

"Just hop on the bed when you're ready," she says. "I'll bring you guys back a cuppa." With an air of authority she disappears out the door.

When she re-enters, the news is not good. She informs me that because my waters have broken I will need to be induced. Watching her set up the drip breaks my heart. I had so dearly wanted a chemical free birth. But the sadness at ripping up my birth plan is soon forgotten as I am plunged into a world of pain. My introduction to the world of contractions begins fast, so fast my tea barely has time to cool.

The hours that follow are a blur of tedious agony. After eating toast, wandering the hospital hallways and discovering my TENS machine is a dud, I take the midwives advice and strip off for a shower. Hauling the IVF cart behind me, I waddle into the bathroom and position myself as best I can on the bright blue birthing ball. Brad squeezes in behind me and turns on the tap.

The warm water brings welcome relief. With one hand on my belly and the other on the drip trolley, I feel disconnected from the world around me. I feel like I am on another plane looking back through a foggy tunnel. I can't believe that I am actually in labour. Me.

As another contraction causes me to double over, I feel the ball begin to slide. Certain I am going to hit the floor, I brace myself. But all of a sudden I am upright. Brad has saved the day. Thinking that the shower may not be my best option right now, he asks what I want to do next. Sobbing I tell him, I just want the pain to stop. That I am tired! That I just want to go home! He tells me he wishes he could do something to help, and I tell him that I can't believe that labour hurts so F@#$ing much!

I want to run out the door, I want everything to go away. But despite my wishes, I am trapped in this never-ending nightmare. For an extraordinarily long time, we do what we have done for the last hour until eventually a nurse arrives and tells me it is time for my next check.

Drying off I lie on the bed and stick out my arm. Within seconds, she confirms what I have already guessed. My blood pressure is rising dramatically. She takes a sample of my blood and tells me I will need medication. Too tired to argue, I roll onto my side and ask Brad to get the iPod.

By noon, I am over it. My blood pressure won't budge and the nurse has returned to top up my drug supply. Watching her refill my IV bag, I ask how long she thinks I still have. In no way am I prepared for her answer.

"Oh, I would say at least another seven hours."

Her answer freezes my world. And it is at that moment I realise there is no way I can do it. I am exhausted. The pain is too much. I can't endure for another seven hours. Like a cornered animal my eyes fleet from Brad to my mum, and then my mouth is moving and the words just fall from my lips. "Any chance you could organise an epidural?"

The moment she leaves I felt better. The contractions don't hurt any less but the knowledge there is a reprieve on the way gives me newfound strength.

Seeing James, the anaesthetist enter the room fifteen minutes later is like seeing an oasis in the desert. I have never been so happy to see another human being. When the drugs begin to take effect, a soft hazy warmth of relaxation washes over me, and I almost weep with gratitude.

4.51 pm

"Hi, Imogen, how are things going?"

I look up to see my obstetrician pulling over the blood pressure monitor.

"Pretty good now," I reply gleefully. "I should have had the epidural earlier."

"They all say that." She laughs. "The good news is that your blood pressure is down. So let's do a quick exam and see how much longer you have to wait."

Awesome, natural birth is back on the table.

"You're ten centimetres dilated." She smiles, tossing the gloves aside. "We are ready to go."

Well, you might be...!

5.15 pm

Fiddling with the drip, the doctor informs me she is turning down the epidural to give me some feeling back. I want to scream, *oh God. No. Don't do that!* But instead I manage a wobbly smile and grip the handrails in anticipation.

"Are you okay?" the doctor asks, adjusting my robe.

"Yeah," I reply, the lie quickly falling from my lips. "I'm good."

"Okay then, let's start."

Oh, this is going to hurt.

Pushing as hard as I can I am surprised at the distinct lack of pain. I know I should say something but fear stops me.

6.35 pm

"That's it, Imogen, one more push and she will be here."

Smiling at Mum, I squeeze Brad's hand and do as I am asked.

6.37 pm

Wahhhhhh!

She's here! I did it! It's over!

As the doctor lifts Paige over the sheet my heart skips a beat. "Imogen, you have a beautiful healthy daughter."

Looking pleased with herself even though I did all the work, she asks the new father if he would like the honours. As I watch Brad take the scissors and snip the cord, I glance my mother's way. She is crying.

"Oh ... Midgey," she sniffles happily. "She is beautiful."

Overjoyed, I turn back to the nurse and am delighted to see her place Paige on my chest, draped in a warm blanket. I put a hand on her silk-like skin and we both lie quietly, staring into each other's eyes.

"Hello, there ... little one," I whisper. "I'm your mummy."

As my new little princess blinks and opens her tiny mouth to yawn, I feel a remarkable sense of relief and overwhelming feelings of love. Looking at her face is like looking into a mirror. Just seeing her, I understand why they say it is all worth it! Now that I have locked eyes with my daughter, I know in my heart that having her was the right decision. I am vaguely aware of the medical staff leaving for the next patient, though I am more interested in the amazing new life in front of me than I am in saying goodbye.

Abandoned like yesterday's news, the emptiness allows us a chance to bond and the whole family is quiet and at peace. Lying back on sweat drenched pillows, I congratulate myself on making it through. *Wow, I did it. I have a family!*

Suddenly realising that I am completely monopolising our new addition, I turn to Brad and smile. "Do you want a hold?"

"Of course!" he laughs. "I thought you would never ask."

Holding her close and watching her every move, I can tell that like me, he is in complete awe of his new daughter. Neither of us can take our eyes off her. It is like watching a tiny angel bathed in moonlight. As the first moments of our new family's life are etched into time, I look at this perfect little creature we have created and shake my head. *Wow, I can't believe I nearly didn't have you.* As a small clog in my heart clicks into place, I feel content.

My world is now complete.

PART THREE

WHAT? BOTTLES WITHOUT BUBBLES

The view from here

Chapter 11

The View From Here

The initiation: forty days and endless nights

When I was expecting, people liked to tell me about the infamous first six weeks—and it was never with a smile brought on by happy memories. Instead, it was accompanied by a look of fatigue, and a strong sense of relief that those times were over. From chatting with everyone from friends to strangers in the checkout queue, I learnt quickly that, despite the joy of welcoming a new baby, the initiation into parenthood could often resemble an extinction event.

Since I had heard all the newborn horror stories, I felt about as mentally prepared as I could be. Having already lived through enough stressful situations, I believed I had the grounding needed to handle most things. In addition, for my entire adult life I had suffered with chronic insomnia and had learnt through sheer necessity how to cope with emotionally draining situations on little to no sleep. Time and again I had proven that, through sheer persistence alone, a person could function for days or even years at a time without adequate rest. I had assumed that these experiences would give me a head start on most new parents. I believed that *I* could handle it.

I was wrong. It didn't take me long to learn that becoming a mother for the first time is like sticking a knife into a toaster: it is shocking, and the pain is immediate. After all my speculation, I discovered that absolutely nothing I had experienced, no matter how difficult, overwhelming, or character-building, could have prepared me for the absolute bombshell that hit when my baby arrived.

Most important milestones in your life come with some sort of training and support, be it from teachers or parents or some other knowledgeable person. Then before advancing in education or taking on a new job, we usually have to study, past tests, or gain relevant experience. Not so with parenthood. The most profoundly difficult task that any person will ever undertake does not come with an instruction manual, nor are we required to have any proven prior knowledge or experience for the job. Aside from family support (if you are so lucky), once that baby comes you are on your own.

When I first arrived home, the sleep deprivation was tough and my body hurt. But despite a fair bit of crying, my baby developed a reasonable and relatively manageable little routine, and we had some lovely moments together. Motherhood seemed exhausting but nice, and like most mothers, I was lulled into a false sense of security. I started thinking, *hey, I can actually do this.*

But then it came. The revelation that all the "just want to help" parents had somehow failed to mention became my rude reality: the moment when my baby "woke up" and didn't want to go back to sleep, ever! And that's when I realised that the expression "sleeping like a baby" has no basis in reality.

Suddenly I was plunged into a world in which my baby was always awake and I got only three hours sleep a night—and that wasn't even the problem. The problem was that when awake, my baby, like most newborns, was rarely satisfied. In fact, my daughter was downright angry about being in this horrible cold loud world and was not the least bit shy about telling me. And once that precious little child of mine started screaming, she just didn't stop. Nothing on earth could have prepared me for the sheer volume of crying, nor did I ever imagine that something so small and innocent could scream so loudly and for so long.

Of course, every mother will have a different experience, and many will have a much easier and calmer initiation into motherhood than I had. It just so happens that mine was tough. It was so tough that at one point a sympathetic lasagne-wielding neighbour was the only thing that saved me from falling completely into an extraordinarily dark abyss, created by a five-hour crying session.

Luckily, though, early motherhood isn't all bad. Sure, your body is tired and sore, and there are days when you feel lost, lonely, and desperate. But then there are plenty of beautiful rays of sunlight mixed in with those dark clouds to help balance things out.

Yes, you might live in a fog of sleep deprivation but becoming a mother is pretty amazing. After nine months of waiting, I finally got to enjoy the fun and revel in the special attention a new baby brings. In those early days, I don't know how many times I sat looking at my little girl, just watching her take in her surroundings or play with her tiny fingers and toes. I remember days when she would gently stroke my face with her sweet chubby hands, or look at me with such complete trust and uncompromising love that my heart would melt. At those times, I could not have been happier. I often wondered if a child could be damaged by too many kisses.

The first weeks of motherhood are monumental and the feelings I experienced as I fell in love with my baby are indescribable. Whilst the difficulties are something that potential mums should be aware of, they certainly shouldn't become a deal breaker. Early on, a friend of Brad's told him, "Mate, you may not believe this, but you will actually live through this." We weren't sure about that at the time but, of course, he was right. Like the millions before us and the millions yet to come, we did make it through to the other side, and if you make this decision so will you.

Six new moons and a baby spoon

Doesn't time fly? One minute I was whinging about a pregnancy that would not end, and the next my baby is six months old and I am a mother. I no longer have to wonder if I will know what to do or how I will manage: I'm doing it and I'm managing. I can now change nappies whilst talking on the phone, breastfeed whilst stirring the dinner and recite the words of "Hush-a-Bye, Baby"—all eight verses—as I pace the bedroom floor.

The past six months have been nothing short of a roller coaster ride. The days and nights have rolled into one long day which has sped past as quickly as a morning at the spa. Now that the early days of two feeds per hour and the crazy nightly crying sessions are behind us, we love being parents. We still have many new things to learn and many years of challenges ahead of us but we finally feel confident as parents. We can happily pack up the car or go away for a day or a weekend without worrying the world might end because we forgot the wipes. Most of the time, we can work out what the crying is for, and we are blessed with our little girl sleeping through the night at least half of the time.

Despite all the concerns I had before my baby arrived, I have been both surprised and pleased as to just how naturally much of parenting has come either from instinct or memories from my childhood. And with the Internet, mothers' groups, or anyone with a pram to ask, I know I'll always find someone to answer my questions.

As expected, there has been a whole new way of life to adapt to. No longer can I just pop down to the store if I have run out of eggs, and we now have to plan our days around meal and nap times. I do miss not being in charge of my day. It seems forever since I could wander aimlessly, not knowing the time and not caring, however, with each week that passes; our new way of life becomes more normal. Whilst we both miss the freedom and peace and quiet that comes with the simple and chaos-free life of a D.I.N.K. (Dual Income No Kids) household, we are learning to share ourselves and be less selfish with our time.

Some days it is still hard to cope with all the added responsibilities. There is the constant worry, the constant supervision, and the reality that everything now takes three times as long as it once did. But at the same time nothing makes a lousy day better than a cuddle, a kiss, and a beautiful baby chuckle from my precious little bundle.

We have also had to adapt to the changes in our relationship now that we are no longer just partners, but also parents. Where there were two, there are now three. The very structure of our relationship has changed, which means that we have lost some of the quality time we once spent together. It has become routine for us to go days without actually catching up and we have forgotten what it is like to have an uninterrupted conversation.

That said, we did go in with our eyes open and knew that a baby would change things, so we are learning to work around these changes. And, even though our relationship has lost some of its intimacy and spontaneity, other areas have grown and strengthened now that we are a family and will continue to develop along with our daughter.

As for our social life, I would be lying if I said we didn't miss our concerts and romantic weekend getaways. And I am still getting used to waiting for the blockbusters to come out on DVD. But despite missing out on some of the things we used to enjoy, our life is now filled with lovely days spent together as a family. Every day I wake up looking forward to seeing my daughter and watching her grow. It is exciting thinking of new things to show her and planning new experiences for us all to share. Whilst we have missed a few celebrations with the old crowd, we have made some fantastic new friends and are enjoying a new, if slightly different, social life. I now know what people mean when they say, "It is still good, just different."

Some of my life dreams, like backpacking around Europe, are on hold, while others have merely been "remodelled". We are now talking about renting a villa in Tuscany with the whole family, once the two new additions are a little older. Two new additions, you may ask? Yes, that's right. My sister Abbey gave birth to a beautiful baby boy, Tyler. So we now have more than one reason to hang around the toddler pools. And I have someone close to my heart who understands all too well the nostalgic look I give the beer garden as we push our prams down to the undercover playground on a bright Sunday afternoon.

Motherhood without the parachute

Motherhood is a lot like jumping out of an aeroplane: it is a state of being that cannot be described but only experienced. And whilst I am convinced that skydiving is an incredible experience, I still haven't found anyone who could adequately describe it in enough detail to make me want to do it.

The bottom line is that I do love being a mother, despite the hardships—and yes, there are many. Motherhood is hard. It is relentless. It is busy. It is stressful. It is exhausting. You must be alert every waking moment. You are always aware of someone else's safety and wellbeing. There is hardly a minute in the day when there isn't something to be done. Motherhood is ten times worse than you imagined and ten times better than you imagined.

What is most challenging about being a parent is not looking after a child. In general, I don't find it difficult or stressful to take care of my daughter. It isn't a hassle to feed, dress, and care for her everyday needs. And when we are playing, reading, or just chatting, it is fun and I am happy and relaxed.

What *is* difficult and stressful is looking after a child *while* trying to fit in all the mundane tasks that must be done, especially if something must be done by a particular time, be it making dinner, getting to an appointment, or putting my daughter to bed at a reasonable hour. Children have no concept of time, so when I am trying to get something done and my child interrupts me, distracts me, or simply goes at a snail's pace when I'm in a hurry, that is when I feel stressed. That is when parenting seems hard. If I never had anything important to do or any kind of time constraints then being a parent would mostly be a breeze. Becoming a mother has certainly given me a real appreciation for the value of time, and I can't believe how much of it I wasted before I had a baby.

I've come to think of motherhood as like hosting a big party. Whilst I do have fun, I find that the night flies and that I have barely enough time to spend with my friends. I forget to eat, forget to dance, and stay up cleaning until the wee hours after sending everyone home with a "Please don't do a thing. Go home to bed". As tired as I am, I'm pleased that my hard work and effort will be appreciated for years to come.

Like a great party, raising a family involves loads of time, effort, and organisation but it also enriches your life. Children, it turns out, are a gift.

I know a few older people who don't have kids. They can sleep in on Sundays, purchase the latest coffee machine, and go on more vacations than I can, and whilst they appear happy, to me their lives seem a little empty. For all the effort, children are worth it. You may have wrestled a screaming baby for twenty minutes but once she closes her eyes and you look down at her angelic slumbering form, your heart melts. It is those moments that make parents glad they took a chance on a baby instead of an espresso machine.

Lessons learnt

Before my journey commenced, I was like a gung-ho teenager who thought she knew everything there was to know about the world, including what being a parent would be like. But what this journey has taught me is that there was no way I could have understood what motherhood really entailed until I had experienced it myself.

I have to admit that I had never paid much attention when I heard women say that. My entire concept of motherhood was based on my imagination and the observed experiences of my friends and my own mother. I had seen them slide down slippery dips, knowing they were offering a prime view of their underwear. I had seen designer shirts ruined from wiping all kinds of disgusting things off little faces. I had seen the tantrums and heard the stories of sleep deprivation. I knew of the never-ending sacrifices. And I knew that from the outside, parenthood looked really unappealing.

But the most important thing I have learnt is that it was a mistake to base my decision about having a family solely on my observations of other people's experiences, and on my own limited experience of taking care of other people's children. What I didn't understand then is that being a parent isn't just about getting all the housework done and keeping track of doctors' appointments, play dates, and swimming lessons. What I discovered is that being a parent is mostly about love. Not just the sort of love you know now, but the kind of love that comes straight from the soul. I'm talking about loving another person so much that you really would do absolutely anything for them. And I mean anything!

Do you remember falling in love for the first time—and falling hard? Do you remember how you felt during those honeymoon days, when you would miss your beloved the moment he left the room? Do you recall a time when you would dye your hair, get a tattoo, or move halfway across the world if only he asked? Or a time, when missing the party of the century seemed a small price to pay in order to spend a few hours alone together snuggling on the couch.

If you can remember the depth of those feelings and can imagine multiplying them by a thousand, then you may begin to understand what a mother's love feels like. You may begin to comprehend why every horrible thing you have imagined about becoming a parent suddenly becomes irrelevant the moment you lock eyes with your child for the first time. It is this exhilaration and never-ending supply of love that makes every compromise and sacrifice worth it and makes motherhood the most incredible and challenging experience in the world.

When you are on the outside looking in, it is almost impossible to be convinced that motherhood will be its own reward. I mean, let's face it; on paper motherhood just isn't that attractive. But like an Olympic gold medallist, you have to believe that all the hard work and sacrifices are worth it. You have to trust that all the early starts, late finishes, aches, pains, and heartaches do fade away once you hold your prize. And in this case, the prize will be your own flesh and blood. All the things that made parenting so unappealing don't bother me at all, and raising my own child is very different from what I imagined it would be like after watching others raise theirs. It is like a magical button is pressed the day you give birth, and all of a sudden everything is okay and it all makes sense.

Another interesting thing I discovered is that whilst becoming a parent is a life-changing event, your transformation into a capable and "normal" mum is slow and gradual. You have time to get used to it. Before I got pregnant, I bumped into an old friend, Jessie, whom I hadn't seen in years. It was great hearing about everything she had been doing over the past decade, including getting married and becoming a mum.

But whilst we were chatting, her kids were running all over the café, getting into all sorts of mischief and interrupting us every two minutes. Jessie seemed so relaxed and capable and the noise and chaos didn't appear to bother her, whilst I found the whole experience overwhelming. As the conversation continued and she chopped her sandwich into tiny bite-size pieces, I wondered how she had gone from fun-loving and fancy-free rat-bag to sensible mother of two, with another on the way. Her transition seemed sudden to me. She was so calm and organised that I figured she was just one of those special women with "born to mother" qualities that I apparently lacked.

It was only after I had my baby that I realised Jessie wasn't unique and that her transition had been gradual. In effect, she grew into her mum role as her kids grew. She had time to get used to them and time to learn how to be a mother. The transformation is like aging: you don't notice the subtle changes taking place each day—it's just a natural progression from stage to stage.

This revelation and so many others have since become apparent to me now that I am on the other side looking back. It took stepping through the door into this new world for me to see what it was all about. I finally understand that I had spent too much time worrying about what it *may* be like instead of just deciding whether I was open to change in my life.

How I feel now

In the words of Elizabeth Stone, "Making the decision to have a child is momentous. It is to decide forever to have your heart go walking around outside your body."

Becoming a mother has changed me in some of the deepest and most marvellous ways imaginable. Before having a child, I wasn't the crying type but now if you ask me how much I love my daughter, just the thought of her will bring tears to my eyes. My new protective motherly instincts mean my emotions are only a breath away. I have such empathy for children now that if I read or hear something on the news about a child being injured or dying, I find tears welling in my eyes. It makes me want to hug my daughter and never let her go. Of course, I thought that sort of stuff was awful even before I had a baby but now it seems to affect me directly and personally. Something changes in your brain when you become a mother and any tragedy real or imaginary can invoke emotions you never knew existed.

Motherhood has also made me a calmer person on the inside and I am definitely more patient and forgiving of others. I feel a sense of fulfilment that I never could have imagined, and have finally found the best reason of all to always be busy, tired, and totally unorganised.

The dark clouds that followed me before and during the pregnancy and during those first few weeks have parted. More than a year has passed and we now see parenthood for the beautiful thing that it can be. There are still tough times and always will be but we couldn't be happier with our decision and we refer to our daughter Paige as "joy". When we tell people that we couldn't imagine life without her, we mean every word.

My initial fears about work and health turned out to be unfounded as well. A week after starting my maternity leave, I was too busy to worry about my job and realised that it would be there when I got back. And honestly, if I didn't need the money I would be quite happy to become a full-time mum, exchanging my career aspirations for baking cookies, face painting, and mothers' groups. We have adapted to less income and our restricted lifestyle alone saves us money.

My concerns about being selfish and not wanting to spend my weekends at dance lessons and making volcanos out of papier-mâché, well, they're laughable. Not only am I learning to live with more chaos and become more patient, I have discovered that all those child-centric activities I previously thought were as exciting as watching the federal budget be handed down, are actually really interesting. Now that I have my own flesh and blood, I can't wait to go to dance recitals and to dip my hands in the glue. And of course, I have a new HD video camera so I can capture every moment and watch them over and over on those quiet Friday nights at home with the family.

One of the biggest questions I had before becoming a parent was, *will I be able to cope?* If you are asking yourself the same thing, I'm here to tell you that the answer is yes. Even when you hit a rough patch and think you can't do one more thing, your maternal instincts will always kick in and you'll do what needs to be done. Those instincts come with an extra supply of energy, with even more boosts provided by the mere sight of your precious baby.

And yes, sometimes it does feel too hard. Sometimes I feel like I am only minutes away from packing my bags and fleeing to the other side of the world but then things change dramatically and quickly. One minute I may be crying and screaming at the heavens, and the next will be rolling around on the floor laughing and having the time of my life. I understand now that I can count on having one bad hour a day, one bad day a week, and, every now and again, just one downright horrible week. But I can also count on the joy and happiness that fill every other part of my daily life.

Final thoughts

So ends the first chapter of this journey. It wasn't so long ago that I was blissfully living my life as a happy carefree woman whose biggest problem was deciding whether her wine should be red or white. Now, just a few years later, here I am in a position to use my experience to help other women find a solution to the decision of a lifetime.

Parenthood is rife with highs and lows, and the pros and cons are so intense and life-changing that I doubt anyone can make a definitive decision without a little doubt and risk either way. As someone who has been there, I recommend that you ask yourself some honest questions and then look into your heart and find the answers there. Ultimately, the only real question is, *will I be happier with children or without them?* I never imagined myself as a mother yet I can honestly say that, despite the hardships, motherhood has been more satisfying and more enriching to my life than any other experience I have ever had. That deep dark void I could never seem to fill in my youth now overflows with love for my new family.

It is with bated breath that I wait to show my daughter the world and be there to experience with her everything the universe has to offer and to rediscover all its joys and wonders through her eyes. Now I have graduations and weddings to look forward to, and—if my daughter wants to take that road—one day I will get the grandchildren I now dream of.

I have also come to realise that whilst we parents may bitch, moan, and complain about how tired we are, and whinge how we haven't had any time to ourselves in years, we honestly wouldn't change things for the world. Now that I know what motherhood is, I know in my heart that if I had chosen to be childfree, I would have absolutely lived to regret it. I understand now why the sacrifices are worth it. I know now that love truly does conquer all.

I hope you have enjoyed following my journey and that I have provided you with some important questions to think about. I have told you my story as honestly as I can. Yes, I could have filled these pages with all those delightful "mother moments" that I now live for but I know what you really need and want is the truth told by a person just like you. I hope I have given you that.

If you do decide to dump your carefree life and jump on board the baby boat, then please see the beginning of this book for details on my website and blog. My website, *babyboat.com.au,* provides lots of information on everything from budgeting and gender selection to preconception care, as well as ongoing insight into life as a 21st-century mum.

Before I send you on your merry way, let me try to wrap up this journey for you as best as I can in a few lines.

Do I miss my abdominals? You bet!

Do I miss my pre-baby life? Every day!

Am I tired? Exhausted doesn't even come close to covering it!

Do I have bad days? All the time!

Do I regret it? No way!

Do I recommend it?

If you have read my book, thought carefully about everything we have discussed, and actually understand just what you might be getting yourself into, and are still interested. Then, the answer is YES! Definitely DO IT!

Now stop procrastinating! Put down that glass of Chardonnay, slip on those sensible shoes, and climb aboard the baby boat.

We're pulling out!

Are you coming?

About the Author

Imogen has a background in human services and has been employed by the University of Queensland's Faculty of Science (*predominantly Biological Sciences*) for over ten years. She is a member of the Queensland Writers Centre (QWC), the founder and CEO of the successful parenting website *babyboat.com.au*, an active blogger, as well as, and most importantly, a full-time mother of two.

She is a lover of life ... Of learning … Of understanding how the world feels to other people. Her aim is to provide mums, mums-to-be and those still deciding with friendly and practical parenting and pregnancy advice, tips and real world support and information.

She has an appreciation for all things that inspire or make us feel normal … And loves anything that is cute, stylish, delicious or ridiculous – as long as it makes her smile.

Connect with the Author

Thank you so much for taking the time to read this book. And I wish you luck on your journey towards making a decision about whether or not having a baby is the right thing for you.

If you have any questions, or want to provide any feedback please feel free to contact me directly at *info@babyboat.com.au*

You can follow me on Twitter:

https://twitter.com/babyauthor1.

And connect with me on Facebook:

https://www.facebook.com/babyboat1.

You can also check out my blog here:

http://babyboat.com.au/blog/.

Or join a special facebook group just for readers like you who are struggling with the baby decision:

https://www.facebook.com/BoardingTheBabyBoatBook.

I wish you the best of health, happiness and success which ever path you take.

Happy Days and Peaceful Nights.

Imogen...